After the Empire

MARK HITCHCOCK

AFTER THE EMPIRE

Tyndale House Publishers, Inc.
WHEATON, ILLINOIS

Cover art by Jane Joseph

Published in 1992 as *After the Empire* by Hearthstone Publishing, Ltd.

Library of Congress Cataloging-in-Publication Data

Hitchcock, Mark.
      After the empire / Mark Hitchcock.
         p.   cm.
      Includes bibliographical references.
      ISBN 0-8423-1656-6
       1. Bible—Prophecies—Russia (Federation)   I. Title.
      BS649.R9H58   1994
      236'.9—dc20   94-10635

Printed in the United States of America

00 99 98 97 96 95 94
8   7   6   5   4   3   2   1

To my parents, who from the day of my birth have pointed me to the Lamb of God who takes away the sin of the world (2 Tim. 3:14-15). Thank you for your wise instruction and consistent example of a life that is well pleasing to the Lord.

TABLE OF CONTENTS

FOREWORD

Students of prophecy have long recognized that Russia will play a significant role in the events of the period immediately preceding the Lord's return to this earth to establish his millennial kingdom. The dissolution of the former Soviet Union has raised questions in the minds of many as to whether the accepted interpretation of passages such as Ezekiel 38 and Daniel 11 still holds true.

The writer of this present volume became interested in the study of prophetic Scriptures during his years of study at Dallas Theological Seminary. To fulfill requirements for the master of theology degree, he wrote a thesis on the king of the north in Daniel 11:40. Since graduation he has continued these studies and is presenting his insights into and conclusions concerning the role the former Soviet Union will play in God's prophetic program. It is his conviction that, instead of requiring a change in interpretation, the changes in the political situation in the former Soviet Union have not only supported the interpretation but have made it easier to understand what Ezekiel and Daniel have predicted.

To all who study prophecy and are interested in the role of the former Soviet Union in prophecy, this work by Mark Hitchcock is highly recommended.

J. Dwight Pentecost
Distinguished Professor of Bible Exposition, Emeritus
Dallas Theological Seminary
Dallas, Texas

The last several years have been years of tremendous political, economic, and social upheaval throughout the world. The Berlin Wall has come crashing down, the entire world was embroiled in the Persian Gulf crisis, and the riots in Los Angeles have brought man's lawlessness and brutality to the forefront. However, no event has shaken the world in the last twenty years like the fall of the Soviet Union. The great Russian bear has fallen, and the attention of the entire world has been riveted on Russia ever since fall 1991 and the attempted coup against Mikhail Gorbachev. The news media throughout the world continues to focus their attention every day on the events in the former Soviet Union. The dissolution of the Soviet Union has sent shock waves through the economic and political waters of this world.

The events in the former Soviet Union in the last few years have also sent shock waves throughout the arena of Bible prophecy interpretation. For many years students of Bible prophecy have taught that the Soviet Union, along with her many allies, would invade the land of Israel in the end times. The recent dramatic changes in the Soviet Union have led many to reexamine how, or even if, Russia fits into God's prophetic program for the nations. When I was in Dallas a few months ago, I saw a copy of a letter from a man in eastern Texas scoffing and ridiculing anyone who ever taught that the Soviet Union would invade Israel. He said that the fall of the Soviet Union showed that he had been right all along and that Russia would never invade Israel. Others have simply changed their view and totally written off the former Soviet Union's part in prophecy altogether. Some are now saying that the Soviet Union must be reunited for God's Word to be literally fulfilled. Even people with little or no interest in Bible prophecy have begun to consider what the Bible has to say about the future of the former Soviet Union and the world.

How are we to understand what's happening? What are we to make of the recent events in the former Soviet Union as they relate to Bible prophecy? How are we to interpret Bible prophecy in light of the dissolution of the Soviet Union? Is God's Word untrue? Have careful, trusted scholars totally missed the mark in interpreting the Bible? Does the Bible have anything to say about the future of the former Soviet republics and the other nations of this world?

The clearest passage in the Bible concerning the place of the former Soviet Union in Bible prophecy is Ezekiel 38 and 39. This passage is one of the most amazing, yet difficult, prophecies in the Bible. These chapters, if interpreted literally, predict an invasion of Israel in the end times by a great northern confederacy of nations accompanied by nations from the south, east, and west of Israel. Ezekiel the prophet predicted this invasion twenty-six hundred years ago, and it has never been literally fulfilled. How can a man predict events over twenty-six hundred years in advance? He can't! Man cannot predict the future. In order to predict the future one must be omniscient, that is, he must know everything, and he must be omnipotent, that is, he must be able to control everything. The only ones who can accurately predict the future are the one true God and his spokesman, the prophet. The prophet Ezekiel is one of God's spokesmen who received revelation directly from God concerning the last days. Seven times in Ezekiel 38 and 39 the phrase "Thus says the Lord GOD" is repeated. In Ezekiel 39:8 it says, "'Behold, it is coming and it shall be done,' declares the Lord GOD." The words of Ezekiel are the very words of God and will therefore be accomplished.

The ability to accurately predict the future is one great fact that separates the false prophet from the true prophet and the false god from the true God. Only the true God can predict the future. "'Remember the former things long past, For I am God, and there is no other; *I am* God, and there is no one like Me, Declaring the end from the beginning And from ancient times things which have not been done, Saying, "My purpose will be established, And I will accomplish all My good pleasure"'" (Isa. 46:9-10).

God is so certain that only he can predict the future that he issues a challenge to the false gods to try to predict the future. "'Present your case,' the LORD says. 'Bring forward your strong *arguments,*' the King of Jacob says. Let them bring forth and declare to us what is going to take place; As for the former *events,* declare what they *were,* That we may consider them, and know their outcome; Or announce to us what is coming. Declare the things that are going to come afterward, That we may know that you are gods" (Isa. 41:21-23).

Since God and God alone is the true source of information about the future of this world, we must look to him for answers concerning the future of the former Soviet republics. The purpose of this book, therefore, is to take a fresh look at Ezekiel 38 and 39 and to let the true God speak. Join with me as we consider what God has to say about the future of the former Soviet Union and the coming invasion of Israel.

ONE

The End of an Empire

If anyone believes that our smiles involve aban-
donment of the teaching of Marx, Engels, and
Lenin, he deceives himself. Those who wait for
that must wait until a shrimp learns to whistle.
— Nikita Khrushchev, speech in Moscow,
September 17, 1955

On Thursday, December 21, 1991, the shrimp learned
to whistle. The unthinkable occurred! The mighty Soviet
Union as we had known it for seventy years no longer
existed. The empire had fallen! All that remains of the
mighty Soviet Empire is a loose commonwealth of the former republics. In the place of the world's most powerful
communist state, there are now fifteen new countries
with individual economic, political, and cultural agendas.

The world has watched these events with great antici-
pation and approval. The greatest threat to the free world

has finally met its demise. The empire of Lenin and Stalin has crumbled. Most people believe that the world is now a safer place.

However, is there more to the fall of the Soviet Union than just the removal of public enemy number one? Does the fall of the Soviet Union have any significance to God's prophetic program for this world? The answer to both of these questions is a resounding yes!

Two monumental results of the fall of the Soviet Union have propelled the world closer to the fulfillment of the events outlined in the Bible in Ezekiel 38–39.

First, the fall of the Soviet Union has left Russia with a devastated economy and a humiliated national ego. With the current rise of nationalist fervor, Russia is more dangerous than ever before.

Second, the fall of the Soviet Union has also left a great power vacuum in central Asia and the Middle East, and this vacuum is being filled by a militant fundamentalist Islam. I believe that these events are happening in preparation for the great invasion of Israel in the end times foretold by the Jewish prophet Ezekiel twenty-six hundred years ago.

The BEAR Necessities

The dissolution of the Soviet Union and the resulting "reforms" have plunged Russia into an economic and political tailspin. The Great Depression in the United States in the 1930s pales in comparison to the present situation in Russia. Food shortages, hyperinflation, diseases, plagues, and environmental disasters are ravaging the Russian bear. Current conditions in Russia are being equated with the scenario in Germany in the 1930s that catapulted Adolph Hitler to power. As the situation in Russia worsens daily, the nationalists, communists, and hard-liners are gaining momentum. All of the important positions in the Russian government have now been retaken by the communists.

If hyperinflation persists, Russia will undoubtedly elect a hard-liner to the presidency in the 1996 election, assuming the nation will wait that long. If Vladimir Zhirinovsky or another nationalistic leader comes to power in the days ahead, Russia will begin to flex her military muscle in that region again. Zhirinovsky, an avowed anti-Semite, has uttered outrageous statements about his vision for a revived, revitalized Russian Empire. With a man like Zhirinovsky gaining power in Russia and positioning himself for the presidency, there is no doubt that Russia today is more dangerous than ever before—especially for Israel! In chapter 4 we will examine in greater detail the severity of the present conditions in Russia as well as the attitudes and actions of Russia's rising star, Vladimir Zhirinovsky.

The Rise of Islam

The Soviet Empire has ended, but a new empire seems to be rising from its ashes. The new empire is not the new commonwealth or even Russia—the new empire is the great Islamic wave.

Amazing events are occurring in our world today, especially the Muslim world, even as these words are being written. Never before in history have world events changed more suddenly or dramatically from the perspective of Bible prophecy. Never have so many biblically relevant factors converged more clearly.

The southern republics of the former Soviet Union are all Muslim nations except the Ukraine, Armenia, and Georgia. The Muslim nations are Azerbaijan, Kazakhstan, Uzbekistan, Kirghizia, Turkmenistan, and Tajikistan. These six new nations make up 21 percent of the population of the old Soviet Union, a total population of 57 million.

These newly independent nations have three main things in common. First, as already noted, they are all Muslim. Second, they all lack hard currency. Third, they all have nuclear weapons within their boundaries and at their disposal. These three factors are obviously a dangerous combination. The scenario is clear: These six republics could conspire with their Islamic brothers in Iran, Syria, Pakistan, Libya, and Turkey to exchange nuclear devices for hard currency. The common bond that binds them together is their common commitment to destroy Israel.

This scenario is already beginning to develop as we see these new Muslim nations forming alliances with other nations, and many of these Muslim nations are also developing close ties with one another. At least one Muslim nation has purchased nuclear weapons from one of the newly independent Muslim republics. These alliances and activities could be the direct fulfillment of Ezekiel 38–39!

Experts on Middle East affairs are proclaiming a powerful new surge of militant Islam in the Middle East. Judith Miller says:

> But most Arab governments are struggling to contain Islamic pressures and to respond to a widespread desire among their citizens for a more "Islamic" government and society. Even in countries where there is little prospect that Islamic forces will rule in the near future, Islam has become the vocabulary of life, changing the language of politics, aspects of national culture, and ethnic traditions. "To a certain extent, Islamic forces have already won," says Gilles Kepel, a French expert on Islamic extremism. "What we're seeing is the re-Islamization of the entire region, the alteration of basic patterns of life."[1]

Miller also says:

> Militant Islam is once again on the move, shaking the foundations of culture and government in even the most stable Arab states. . . . More than a decade after the first modern Islamic revolution, in Iran, militant Islam is . . . transforming everyday life in the Middle East and challenging the legitimacy of almost every state.[2]

So what is the cause of this sudden rise in militant Islam? Experts agree that two explosive events in the last few years have served as catalysts for the new rise of Islam. These two events are the Persian Gulf War and the collapse of the Soviet Union and communism.[3]

Communism was the strongest opponent to Islam in the Mideast. Therefore, the fall of the Soviet Union has thrown the door wide open for militant Islam to rise like a rocket in the Middle East.

The breakup of the Soviet Union has caused a dramatic power shift that affects every area of the world. The world has not been stabilized by the fall of the Soviet Union; it has been greatly destabilized. Three major factors contributed to the balance of power that existed in the world for several decades:

1. There were only two major players (the U.S. and the Soviet Union);
2. both were in approximate balance; and
3. both were considered rational.[4]

Now the balance of power has been thrown into confusion. There are no longer two players involved in the balance-of-power formula—there are over a dozen. The world is more at risk for a global holocaust than at any time in history. Nuclear weapons are being distributed and are falling into the hands of irrational, fanatical leaders! The fomentation in the Islamic world could ignite at any time into a jihad, or holy war.

The present situation that is developing in the Middle East as a result of the fall of the Soviet Union is best expressed by Mohamed Heikal, Egypt's most prominent spokesman for secular Arab nationalism:

> Because of the failure of the existing regimes, their corruption, bankruptcy, [and] the absence of an alternative, inspiring vision, there is a huge political vacuum. Only Islam makes sense, is authentic, to most Arabs.[5]

A new slogan has become the hallmark of the militant Islamic movement: "Islam is the solution."

The Islamic Threat

Islam is the religion of those who follow the prophet Muhammad who lived in the seventh century. The word Islam means submission, surrender, or commitment; therefore, it describes the proper relationship between God and man. Followers of Islam are known as Moslems or Muslims, that is, "submitters." Their sacred book is the Koran, which allegedly contains the revelations of God (Allah) to his prophet Muhammad.

Islam has emerged as the world's fastest-growing religion with almost two billion followers. The largest Muslim population in the world is in Indonesia, but large numbers of Muslims live in Pakistan, India, Bangladesh, Turkey, Egypt, Sudan, Iran, Nigeria, and the former southern republics of the Soviet Union. The desire of Islamic leadership is to unite all Muslims into a Muslim Crescent extending from Indonesia in the Pacific to northwest Africa in the Atlantic.

Today there are more Muslims in Great Britain than Christians. Over nine hundred churches have been converted into mosques. In the United States there are over three million Muslims. There are more followers of Islam in the United States than Episcopalians, and three times more Muslims than members of the Assemblies of God.

Like all religions, Islam has its sects. In the seventh century the Muslim world split into two great divisions: Sunni and Shia. The vast majority of Muslims today are Sunni. Only 12 percent to 15 percent of all Muslims are Shiites, and they are mainly centered in Iran. The primary difference between the two groups is that in the Sunnis the leaders have less authority. The Shiites believe that leadership is restricted to descendants of Ali, Muhammad's son-in-law.

The modern militant agenda of Islam is startling. The concept of jihad is becoming more and more prevalent. The Islamic doctrine of jihad means an active struggle for the victory of Islam using armed force when necessary. The object of jihad is not primarily the conversion of individuals but the gaining of political control over nations to run them in accordance with the principles of Islam. Jihad against unbelief is considered a religious duty. All true believers are obliged to combat both individuals and their governments who do not adhere to Islamic beliefs.

Militant Islam views the whole world as divided into two

groups: *dar al-islam* and *dar al-harb*. *Dar al-islam* is the realm of submission, or Islam. *Dar al-harb* is the realm of war on those who are not followers of Islam. For Muslims there is no middle ground. One is either a true believer or an infidel, saved or damned, a friend or an enemy of God, a member of God's army or a follower of Satan, and the army of God is locked in a battle or holy war with the followers of Satan! Christians and Jews are both regarded as unbelievers and are viewed as partners in a Judeo-Christian conspiracy against Islam and the Muslim world. That's why both Israel and the United States are the hated enemies of the militant Islamic movement.

Ezekiel the Prophet

Ezekiel 38–39 clearly predicts a great northern invasion of Israel in the last days with the help of many allies. I believe this passage primarily predicts a great Russian-*Islamic* invasion of Israel. The former Russian republic will be involved, but the great impetus for the invasion will be provided by Islamic nations.

All of the names mentioned in Ezekiel 38–39 are presently within the current geographical boundaries of Islamic nations that are rapidly forming alliances with one another. The Soviet Union has fallen, and Islam seems to be moving in to fill the vacuum, and of course all the world knows that no one despises the Jewish state like the Muslims.

However, before we jump to any conclusions about Russia, the former southern republics of the Soviet Union, or other Muslim nations, we must identify the participants in this invasion. Therefore, the first question that must be answered in our study of Ezekiel 38–39 is the "who" question. Who are the specific participants in this invasion?

Chronology of Major Events Before, During, and After the Fall of the Soviet Union

August 1991—Communist hard-liners attempt a coup in Moscow, trying to oust Mikhail Gorbachev from power. After three days the coup fails and Gorbachev is returned briefly to power.

September 1991—Civil war breaks out in the Georgia republic.

December 8, 1991—Leaders of Russia, Byelorussia, and Ukraine meet in the Byelorussian city of Brest to officially declare the end of the U.S.S.R.

December 17, 1991—Mikhail Gorbachev and Boris Yeltsin meet in Moscow to discuss an orderly transition of power. They agree the Soviet Union would cease to exist by 1992.

December 21, 1991—Eleven former Soviet republics meet in the Kazakh city of Alma-Ata and sign an agreement to create a commonwealth.

December 23, 1991—Gorbachev and Yeltsin meet again in the Kremlin to discuss the final transfer of power.

December 25, 1991—Gorbachev officially resigns as president of the U.S.S.R.

December 31, 1991—The Soviet flag atop the Kremlin is officially replaced by the red, white, and blue flag of pre-revolutionary Russia.

February 1, 1992—U.S. President George Bush meets with Boris Yeltsin at Camp David. Together the two leaders declare an end to the cold war and outline new guidelines for future relations between the U.S. and Russia.

February 1992—Uzbekistan, Turkmenistan, Tajikistan, and Kirghizia join together with Iran, Turkey, and Pakistan to form an Islamic common market.

June 1992—Boris Yeltsin and George Bush meet in Washington for a two-day summit on nuclear arms reductions.

October 1993—Boris Yeltsin dissolves the Russian parliament, and hard-liners, led by Alexander Rutskoi, hole up in the parliament building. It is the worst political violence in Moscow since the 1917 Bolshevik Revolution.

December 1, 1993—In a presidential decree, Boris Yeltsin replaces the hammer and sickle with the two-headed eagle as the official government seal of Russia.

December 12, 1993—Russia holds its first popular elections in seventy years. The Liberal Democratic Party, led by Vladimir Zhirinovsky, receives 24 percent of the vote, the most received by any party.

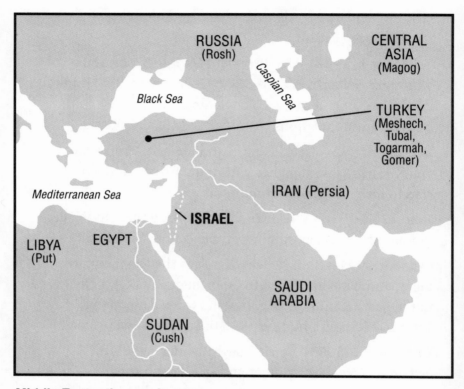

Middle East—then and now

Gog and Magog

WHO are the nations Ezekiel says will invade Israel in the last days? Are the nations that are making alliances with one another possibly fulfilling Ezekiel 38–39? The purpose of the next six chapters is to carefully investigate these questions because, when we know who is involved, we can begin to see that the pieces seem to be rapidly falling into place.

The names listed in Ezekiel 38:2-6 have been identified with many nations including the Soviet Union, Eastern Europe, Germany, and several different African and Arab nations. However, most of the identifications of the names in Ezekiel 38:2-6 have been based on either speculation, simply quoting someone else who agrees with the author's conclusions, or by twisting the locations of the names to fit the current scenario to sensationalize the prophecy.

Therefore, we will begin our study of Ezekiel's great prophecy with a close examination of each of the names in this section. I think you will be amazed at what we find.

God's Top Ten Most Wanted List

At the outset of Ezekiel 38–39, ten names are included in the great horde that will descend upon Israel in the last days:

> And the word of the LORD came to me saying, "Son of man, set your face toward *Gog* of the land of *Magog,* the prince of *Rosh, Meshech,* and *Tubal* . . . *Persia, Ethiopia,* and *Put* with them, all of them *with* shield and helmet; *Gomer* with all its troops; *Beth-togarmah from* the remote parts of the north with all its troops—many peoples with you" (Ezek. 38:1-2, 5-6, emphasis added).

The ten names listed here are God's Top Ten Most Wanted List. God says in Ezekiel 38:3 and 39:1, "I am against you." The God of this universe is against the nations listed in this chapter and he is against their leader. God issues a warrant for their arrest and execution in this chapter. The ten names in this chapter have been tried in the supreme court of this universe and found guilty. All that remains is for the sentence to be executed, and the one who will execute judgment is God himself. God will bring these nations against Israel in the last days to meet their final doom.

The Family Tree of the World

Who are these nations that God says he is against? They don't sound like any nations you would see on a world map today. The reason these names are so unfamiliar is because they were names of people or nations that existed in the days of Ezekiel around 600 B.C. However, this is not the first time these nations are listed in the Bible. All of these names occur in other places in the Bible except the name Rosh, and all of the names except Gog and Rosh are found in Genesis 10, which is often called the Table of the Nations, or the family tree of the world.

In Genesis 10 the descendants of Noah are divided into three great branches on the family tree. The three great branches are Noah's three sons: Shem, Ham, and Japheth. All people trace their ancestry to one of these three men.

The descendants of Shem originally settled in the area of Mesopotamia. Of course, Abraham, the father of the Jewish people, was a descendant of Shem, so Abraham's descendants through his son Isaac inhabited the land of Canaan.

The descendants of Japheth moved to the north after the Flood, eventually populating Asia, Asia Minor, and Europe.

Ham's descendants migrated southward after the Flood. Some of his descendants settled in Mesopotamia and the land of Canaan, but most moved farther south into Arabia and Africa.

With this overview in mind, let's look now at the first two names on God's Top Ten Most Wanted List.

Public Enemies Number 1 and 2

The first two names on God's Top Ten Most Wanted List
are the mysterious and unusual names Gog and Magog.
These two names are often used as a summary of all the
enemies of Israel mentioned in this chapter. Ezekiel 38–
39 are often referred to as the prophecy of Gog and
Magog. Most students of Bible prophecy have identified
Gog and Magog as Russia or the Soviet Union. Therefore,
a proper understanding of these first two names is central
to a proper understanding of Ezekiel 38–39.

The Great Gog

The name Gog only appears once in the Bible outside of
Ezekiel 38–39. In 1 Chronicles 5:4 Gog is listed as one of
the descendants of Reuben. However, the Gog in that passage has no relation to the Gog of Ezekiel. In Ezekiel 38–
39 the name Gog appears eleven times, more than any of
the other invaders. We conclude, therefore, that Gog is
the most important person or nation in this coalition.
God says to Gog, "Son of man, set your face toward *Gog*"
(Ezek. 38:2); "Behold, I am against you, O *Gog*" (Ezek.
38:3); "I shall be sanctified through you before their eyes,
O *Gog*" (Ezek. 38:16); "And it will come about on that
day, when *Gog* comes against the land of Israel" (Ezek.
38:18); "Prophesy against *Gog* . . . '"Behold, I am against
you, O *Gog*"'" (Ezek. 39:1); "I shall give *Gog* a burial
ground there in Israel. . . . So they will bury *Gog* there . . .
and they will call *it* The Valley of Hamon-*Gog*" (Ezek.
39:11); "The valley of Hamon-*Gog*" (Ezek. 39:15, empha-

ses added). Gog is clearly the leading actor in this great drama at the end of the ages. But who is this one the Bible refers to only by the cryptic name Gog?

Many scholars have attempted to identify Gog with various ancient names such as Gyges, the king of ancient Lydia; a king named Gaga; a Babylonian god named Gaga; or an ancient ruler named Gagi. However, none of these suggestions has any support to lead to the conclusion that Gog should be identified with them. So who is Gog?

The name *Gog* means "high, supreme, a height, or a high mountain." The way the name is used in Ezekiel 38–39 certainly reveals that Gog is a person, not a place. Ezekiel says that Gog is "of the land of Magog" and that Gog is the "prince of Rosh, Meshech, and Tubal." This language shows clearly that Gog is a person from the land of Magog who is the prince or ruler of Rosh, Meshech, and Tubal. As Hal Lindsey says in *The Late Great Planet Earth,*

> Gog is the symbolic name of the nation's leader and Magog is his land. He is also the prince of the ancient people who were called Rosh, Meshech, and Tubal.[6]

Most scholars believe that, since Gog means "high or supreme," it is not the person's name but a kingly title like pharaoh, czar, or president. Therefore, the reason Gog is singled out eleven times by God in these two chapters is because Gog is the general over this coalition of nations in its great military campaign against Israel.

We now know that Gog is a person, but the Bible also

gives us information concerning the place from which this coming military ruler will arise. The Bible says in Ezekiel 38:15 and 39:1-2 that Gog comes from the "remotest parts of the north." The general location of Gog's home base, therefore, is in the region that is remotely north from the land of Israel. Interestingly, the word *Caucasus* means "Gog's Fort." *Gog* and *Chasan* ("fort") are the two words from which the word *Caucasus* is derived.[7] The Caucasus mountain range is between the Black and Caspian Seas in the southern part of the former U.S.S.R. This mountain range is named "Gog's Fort!"

The Bible goes on to tell us in Ezekiel 38:2 that Gog comes specifically from the land of Magog. Therefore, to find out the precise place from which Gog arises, we must identify the ancient land of Magog. Magog is the land of Gog!

Meet Magog

As we have already seen, Magog was the second son of Japheth in Genesis 10:2. This is the only time the name Magog appears in the Bible except in 1 Chronicles 1:5, Ezekiel 38:2, and 39:6. Outside the Bible, the name is not found in ancient literature except by those commenting on the Bible.

Ancient Magog has been identified with several groups of people. One ancient scholar named Barabas states that Magog was probably located between ancient Cappadocia (modern Turkey) and ancient Media (modern Iraq and Iran). Medieval writers interpreted Magog as Spain. Ezekiel's prophecy was interpreted as a prediction that Spain would be liberated from the Moors. Other identifications have included the Celts/Galatians, the Parthians, the Huns, the Mongols, the Arabians, the Magyars, and the Turks. However, the most likely identification of Magog is provided by the Jewish historian Josephus who said, "Magog founded the Magogians, thus named after him, but who by the Greeks are called Scythians."[8] This identification was also adopted by the church fathers Jerome and Theodoret. Therefore, if we want to know about Magog, understanding the ancient Scythians is the key.

Who Are the Scythians?

The name Scythian refers to a number of the great northern nomadic tribes who inhabited territory from central Asia all across the southern part of ancient Russia. The word Scythian can be used in both a narrow and a broad sense:

> In the narrow sense, the Scythians were the tribes who lived in the area which Herodotus designated as Scythia (i.e., the territory north of the Black Sea) and who spoke the Scythian language. . . . In the broad sense the word Scythian can designate some of the many other tribes in the vast steppes of Russia, stretching from the Ukraine in the west to the region of Siberia in the east.[9]

Originally, all of the Scythian tribes lived in the area of central Asia, which is located today in the former central

Asian republics of the Soviet Union. However, around 700 B.C. these Scythian hordes came over the Caspian Sea into the area north of the Black Sea (modern Ukraine) and defeated the Cimmerians, driving them into modern Turkey.

In the Persian era, about sixty years after Ezekiel wrote, the Persians divided the Scythians into three groups. The first group was known as the Beyond the Sea Scythians. This group resided in the area to the north of the Black Sea in the modern area of the Ukraine (a former Soviet republic). The second group of Scythians were called Haumavarga Scythians. This name is derived either from the fact that these Scythians ate the hallucinogenic haoma plant or from one of their leaders named Humarga ("he who has good plains").[10] These Scythians were located in central Asia, south of Lake Balkhash. This area today is located within the five former central Asian republics of the U.S.S.R. The third group of Scythians were called the "pointed-hat" Scythians. Most scholars place these Scythians in the east between the Caspian and Aral seas, just west of the Haumavarga Scythians.

Savage Scythians

Ancient history tells us a great deal about the northern nomads called the Scythians. We know that the Scythians were a cruel, warlike people who mastered the art of horsemanship. It has been said that the favorite occupation of the Scythians was war and their favorite companion was their horse. In his book *Foes From the Northern*

Frontier, Edwin Yamauchi provides excellent insight into the culture of these ancient warriors. He says:

> The Scythians were among the most skilled horse-men ever known. It was their superb horsemanship, especially their ability to shoot arrows while riding at a gallop, even at enemies behind them, that gave the Scythians and their later imitators, the Parthians, a distinctive military advantage.[11]

Yamauchi also says:

> The Scythians were among the earliest mounted arch-ers in antiquity. They were certainly among the most skilled, able even to fire backward while riding at a gallop. Such a skill is best learned from childhood. According to Plato (Laws, 795A) the Scythians could shoot as easily with the left as with the right hand. Lucian (Hermotimos, 33) relates that while galloping they were able to hit a moving beast or bird.
>
> Though the Scythians had other weapons such as battle axes, daggers, spears, and swords, they were most wedded to the bow. They would advance quickly, fire their arrows, and retreat before their enemies could engage them.[12]

The best source of information concerning the Scythi-ans has been the ancient historian Herodotus, the "Father of History." He relates many bizarre, cruel, and savage practices of the Scythians:

1. The Scythians drank the blood of the first enemy killed (4.64).
2. They carried the heads of their victims to their chiefs. They scalped their enemies and used these scalps as "napkins" (4.64).
3. They used the skins of their victims to cover their quivers (4.64).
4. They drank from the skulls of their victims (4.65).
5. They practiced blood brotherhood by drinking each other's blood mixed with wine (4.70).
6. The Scythians "bathed" in the vapor from heated hemp seeds (4.75).
7. When their king died, they sacrificed one of his concubines and several servants (4.71).
8. After a year they commemorated his death by sacrificing fifty servants and fifty horses (4.72).

The Greek word *Skuthes*, or "Scythian," occurs in the New Testament. In Colossians 3:11 Paul stresses the fact that all believers in Jesus Christ, regardless of their backgrounds, are one in Christ, *"a renewal* in which there is no *distinction between* Greek and Jew, circumcised and uncircumcised, barbarian, *Scythian,* slave and freeman, but Christ is all, and in all"* (emphasis added). This shows that even in the first century A.D. the Scythians were still considered to be the most savage of all people. Scythians were considered the lowest class of barbarians. The term was applied to the tribes around the Black Sea who were described as "a wretched slave class."[13] Josephus, who also wrote in the first century A.D., said, "The Scythians, they take a pleasure in killing men, and differ little from brute beasts."[14] One especially vile practice of some of the Scythians was that of cannibalism. A deceased person was eaten by his relatives.

Throughout their history, the Scythians are described as a warlike, viciously cruel, barbaric people who inhabited central Asia and the southern part of Russia.

We now have a clearer picture of the identity, culture, and customs of the ancient Scythians. But you are probably wondering at this point what all this has to do with the fall of the Soviet Union and Bible prophecy. Therefore, the questions we must now answer are: Who are the Scythians today? Who are the peoples who inhabit the ancient territory of these barbaric savages today?

Magog Today

The descendants of ancient Magog—the Scythians—were the original inhabitants of the plateau of central Asia, and later some of these people moved into the area north of the Black Sea. The homeland of the ancient Scythians is inhabited today by the former Soviet republics of Kazakhstan, Kirghizia, Uzbekistan, Turkmenistan, Tajikistan, and the Ukraine. All of these former republics, which are now independent nations, are Muslim nations except the Ukraine.

All of the Muslim former republics are being courted by their Islamic neighbors—especially Turkey and Iran. Most importantly, however, is the fact that all of these former republics except Kirghizia have tactical nuclear weapons within their boundaries, and Kazakhstan has not only tactical nuclear weapons but also ICBM (intercontinental ballistic missile) sites and strategic-bomber bases. Some have ranked Kazakhstan as the fourth-greatest nuclear power in the world today.

The rise of militant Islam in the five former central Asian republics is startling. Many of the younger generation of radicals accuse the official Islamic establishment of having collaborated with the godless Soviet regime. These radicals have made their view very clear:

> "It doesn't matter that they are Shiite over there, and we are Sunni," argues a militant in the Uzbek city of Namangan. "The Ayatollah made Iran strong and glorious, while in Sunni Turkey they have weakened Islam." Muslim political aspirations have found a focus in the Islamic Renaissance Party, which held its founding congress in 1990. . . . "Our goals are similar to those of the Iranian revolution. . . . We stand for tradition."[15]

This new militant political party now has chapters in both Uzbekistan and Tajikistan. In another city in Uzbekistan, so many people stream to the mosques during the afternoon prayer that Islamic guards must be used to keep order. The cry that echoes from these mosques is "God is great!"[16] Before independence from the Soviet Union in 1991, there were two hundred

mosques in all of Uzbekistan. Now there are five thousand!

One political expert in this area says:

> The growth of the Islamic movement will be in
> direct proportion to the decline in the region's eco-
> nomic and social conditions. . . . If the West waits
> until tomorrow or the day after to get involved, it
> may be too late.[17]

In other words, if economic conditions get too bad,
these nations are an Islamic powder keg waiting to
explode. With the world's economy like it is today, it's
very likely that the fuse to this powder keg is already
burning!

Conclusion

It is not too difficult to imagine that these Muslim
nations could be drawn into an end-time invasion of
Israel. With the breakup of the former Soviet Union,
these nations are free to act independently of the rest of
the former Soviet republics. We can already see that these
former republics are being heavily courted by both the
Turks and the Iranians and that the seeds of militant
Islam are presently being sown. The great Gog coalition
could be beginning with the dissolution of the Soviet
Union in 1991–92. The fall of the Soviet Union has made
the fulfillment of Ezekiel 38–39 more possible than ever
before.

I hope that you are beginning to see the importance of ancient Magog. His descendants in central Asia are in a better position to fulfill Ezekiel's prophecy than at any previous time in history, and we know that the leader of this great coalition will come from Magog. Remember, Gog is "of the land of Magog." Keep your eyes on the land of Magog, the land of the ancient Scythians, because it is from this land that the great Gog will arise!

But before we say any more about Gog and Magog, let's move on to look at the other participants in this great invasion. The coalition of nations listed in Ezekiel 38:2-6 looks as if it were taken from today's newspapers and magazines!

THREE

Is Rosh Russia?

T HE next name that appears on God's Top Ten Most Wanted List in Ezekiel 38 is Rosh. This name has stirred up more controversy than all the other names in this list put together because of its obvious similarity to the word *Russia*. The similarity of the name Rosh to the modern nation of Russia has led many prophecy students to insist that Rosh is Russia. This identification has been held by many scholars, but the view was greatly popularized by the *Scofield Reference Bible*. Scofield's note on Ezekiel 38:2 says "that the primary reference is to the Northern (European) powers headed up by Russia, all agree."[18] The identification of Rosh with Russia is further bolstered by the mention of the next two names in Ezekiel 38:2, Meshech and Tubal, with the Russian cities of Moscow and Tobolsk. This view thrived in the late 1930s and early 1940s when Russia emerged as a world power and gained even more momentum in the days of the Cold War. In the 1970s and early 1980s, with the Soviet Union's invasion of Afghanistan and close alliance with several Arab nations, it seemed that the invasion in Ezekiel 38–39 was imminent. But the early 1990s have brought monumental changes to the scene that many thought was developing. Iraq has been defeated. The Soviet Union has fallen apart, and many have been left wondering if Rosh has any relation whatsoever to Russia.

The majority of contemporary scholars reject any connection between Rosh and Russia. They think that the only basis for connecting Rosh and Russia is the similarity of sound of the names, and they flatly reject this view.

So what are we to make of this wide difference of opinion? Is there any way to clear the waters, especially since the waters have been muddied by the fall of the Soviet Union? Is Rosh really Russia, or should we look elsewhere for the identity of Rosh?

Rosh: Name or Title?

Before we get to the identity of Rosh, we first have to establish that the word *Rosh* is the name of a geographical location. Many scholars believe that the word *rosh* in Ezekiel 38:2 is not a proper name but is another title describing Gog.

The Hebrew word *rosh* simply means "head, top, summit, upper part, chief, total, or sum." It is a very common word to all Semitic languages. It occurs approximately 750 times in the Old Testament along with its roots and deriva-

tives. The meaning of this word has led many Bible scholars to translate the word *rosh* here not as a proper name but
simply as "chief." They translate Ezekiel 38:2, "the chief
prince of Meshech and Tubal." The King James Version, the
Revised Standard Version, the *New American Bible,* and the
New International Version all adopt this translation.

Three main points support the view that the word *rosh*
in this verse is simply a title. First, no geographic location called Rosh is ever mentioned outside Ezekiel 38–39
in the Old Testament or in literature outside the Bible.
Second, Meshech and Tubal, the next two names in Ezekiel 38:2, are usually mentioned together in Scripture
and are never associated with Rosh within or outside the
Scripture. Third, the accents in the Hebrew text favor the
translation "the prince, the chief of Meshech and Tubal."

While these three arguments are all true, the great
weight of evidence favors taking Rosh as a proper name
of a geographical location. The great Hebrew scholars C.
F. Keil[19] and Wilhelm Gesenius[20] both state clearly that
Rosh in Ezekiel 38:2-3 and 39:1 is a proper name of a
geographical location. The Septuagint, the Greek translation of the Old Testament, translates the Hebrew *rosh* as
the proper name Ros. This point is especially important
since the Septuagint was translated only three centuries
after the book of Ezekiel was written. Many Bible dictionaries and encyclopedias also support this view: the *New
Bible Dictionary,*[21] the *Wycliffe Bible Dictionary,*[22] and the
International Standard Bible Encyclopedia.[23]

Another point in favor of identifying Rosh with a geographical location rather than a title is its recurrence in Ezekiel 38:3 and 39:1. If Rosh was simply a title, it probably would be dropped in these two places because when titles are repeated, they are generally abbreviated.

The most impressive evidence in favor of taking Rosh as a proper name is simply that this translation is the most accurate. G. A. Cooke, a Hebrew scholar, translates the phrase in Ezekiel 38:2 "the chief of Rosh, Meshech, and Tubal." He says, "This is the most natural way of rendering the Hebrew."[24] Another Old Testament scholar, John Taylor, agrees with Cooke that this is the best way to translate the Hebrew.[25] Several translations of the Bible agree. Rosh is translated as a proper name in *The Jerusalem Bible, The New English Bible,* and the *New American Standard Bible.*

Having found that Rosh is a proper name, the next questions we must ask are: To whom or what does the name Rosh refer? Is Rosh Russia or should we look somewhere else? We will answer these questions from two primary sources: the Bible and ancient history.

Rosh in the Bible

The word *Rosh* occurs only four times in the Bible as a proper name. One of the occurrences of the word *Rosh* as a proper name is in Genesis 46:21. Rosh is the name of the seventh son of Benjamin. All three of the remaining occurrences of this word are in Ezekiel (38:2-3; 39:1). Therefore, the best place to begin our study of the identity of Rosh is the immediate context in which it occurs.

In all three of its occurrences, Rosh is listed with Meshech and Tubal under the rule of Gog. The only indication the Bible gives us of the location of these names is that they come from the "remotest parts of the north" (38:15; 39:2).

Two of Gog's other allies, Gomer and Togarmah, are also said to come from the "remotest parts of the north" (38:6). Rosh is linked both militarily and geographically with other nations from the remotest parts of the north. We know, therefore, that seven of the ten nations mentioned in Ezekiel 38:2-6, including Rosh, come from far north.

While this information from the Bible narrows down the general geographical location of Rosh, in order to determine the identity of Rosh more specifically, we must turn to ancient history and sources outside the Bible.

Rosh in Ancient History

The exact name Rosh doesn't appear in documents or inscriptions in ancient history. This has led many Bible scholars to believe that it is impossible to identify Rosh with any certainty. However, there are several names mentioned in ancient history that fit the biblical identification of Rosh. A careful investigation of these names and the ancient people they represent will answer the question: Is Rosh Russia?

The name Russia was not used in ancient history until the tenth century A.D. The name Russian State was not officially adopted until the fifteenth or sixteenth century

A.D. Therefore, the word *Rosh* used by Ezekiel around 585 B.C. does not refer precisely or exactly to Russia because all of the names in Ezekiel 38:2-6 refer to places that existed in Ezekiel's day. To find out if a place called Rosh existed in Ezekiel's day and where that place was, let's look at ancient history.

We have already seen in the last chapter that Magog was the ancient Scythians, a northern tribe of fierce warriors who inhabited central Asia and southern Russia. In the next chapter we will see that Gomer is the ancient Cimmerians, another tribe of northern warriors. Ancient Rosh is a third great group of fierce northerly people called the Sarmatians. In the three names Magog, Gomer, and Rosh, Ezekiel includes the three great groups of people who inhabited the area of central Asia and southern Russia from 1000 B.C. to A.D. 200. We have already looked at the Scythians (Magog) in the last chapter, and we will look at the Cimmerians (Gomer) in the next chapter, but now it's time to study the Sarmatians, the people Ezekiel calls Rosh.

The Sarmatians were an Iranian tribe of nomadic people that inhabited the area around the Caspian Sea in 900 B.C. The Sarmatians were known by the Assyrians as the Ras or Rashu. An ancient Assyrian inscription written about 700 B.C. refers to an attack upon the Rashu of the land of Rashu. The land of Rashu was on the northern border of ancient Elam in the area between the Black and Caspian Seas. T. G. Pinches has noted that the Hebrew spelling of Rosh presupposes an earlier pronunciation as

Rash, a form that agrees closely with the one used by the Assyrians.[26]

Another ancient inscription refers to the ancient people of Rosh, or the Sarmatians. The Babylonian Chronicle in 613–12 B.C. refers to the land of Rasapu. During a northern campaign by the Babylonian king Nabopolassar, he went into the area of Nisibin. Spoil and prisoners from the land of Rasapu were brought before him at Nineveh. The area of Rasapu, like the land of Rashu of the Assyrians, is located in Sarmatia, the area around the Caucasus Mountains between the Black and Caspian Seas. Herodotus confirms this location because he frequently mentions the Sauromatians in book 4 of his *Histories* in connection with military campaigns against Cyrus and the Scythians around 540 B.C. He locates Sauromatia between the Black and Caspian Seas just north of the Caucasus Mountains. This area today is occupied by the former Soviet republics of Armenia, Georgia, and Azerbaijan.

The third and most important link between the ancient Sarmatians and Rosh is found in the word *Rus*. George Vernadsky, the most noted scholar on Russian history in the world, has written several volumes on Russian history. He believes that the word *Rus*, which later became *Russia*, is of Iranian origin and refers to the ancient Sarmatians. Vernadsky says:

> The origin of the name Ros, or Rus, is not definitely established. . . . Personally, I incline to a different explanation of the name. As we have seen, the Sarmatian

tribes of Aorsi and Roxolani spread as early as the second century B.C. over the area of the Volga, Dan, Donets, and Dnieper rivers. The names of these tribes may be derived from the Iranian words *ors, uors* ("white"), and *rukhs* ("light"). . . . As we know, one of the clans of the Iranian Antes, or As, was known as the Light As (Rukhs-As). Later, the Slavic tribes subordinated to the Rukhs clan must have assumed this name. . . . The original Rukhs might in some local dialects, Slavic among others, sound as *Rohs, Ross,* or *Rus,* in light of which the origins of the Greek *Ros* and Slavic *Rus* may be understood.[27]

In another of his books, Vernadsky says:

At the beginning of the fourth century B.C. another Iranian people, the Sarmatians, began to press upon the Scythians, and by the end of the second century B.C. they had occupied the shores of the Black Sea. Among the Sarmatians the most powerful tribe was the Alans who, until the coming of the Huns, were considered the best horsemen of the steppes. . . . One clan was known as the Rukh-As—"the light (or brilliant) Alans," and it is from this name that *Ros* or *Rus* (hence, Russia, Russians) presumably derives.[28]

Several other scholars have also observed the connection between the Sarmatians and Rosh. Louis S. Bauman in his book *Russian Events in the Light of Bible Prophecy* says:

Historians agree that the Magogites were divided into two distinct races, one Japhetic, or European, and the other Turanian, or Asiatic.

The Japhetic race comprised those whom the Greeks and Romans call Sarmatians, but who, in modern times, are called Slavs or Russians. The Sarmatians were a mixture of Medes and Scythians who coalesced and emigrated in small bands into the regions north of the Black Sea and extending from the Baltic Sea to the Ural Mountains.

The Turanian race comprised those Asiatic Magogites (Scythians) who dwelt upon the great plateau of central Asia, from whence they emigrated and spread out over the immense plain of northern Asia and northern Europe. Today their descendants are known as Tartars, Cossacks, Finns, Kalmuks, and Mongols.[29]

The article on Rosh in the *Wycliffe Bible Dictionary* says, "However, the name of a third northerly people is more likely. Rosh was probably one of the Sarmatian or Iranian tribes around the Caspian Sea."[30] Another writer joins this identification:

> Our hypothesis is, then, that Rosh was one of the many Sarmatian or Iranian tribes which almost surrounded the Caspian Sea; was located near the Caucasus Mountains perhaps as early as the tenth century B.C. . . . Rosh, or Rus, was part of the migration of its sister tribes from farther east, which went into the Crimea and Caucasus areas.[31]

We see from this that ancient Magog was the Scythians who came from central Asia and spread into southern Russia around 700 B.C. We also see that ancient Rosh was the Sarmatians who inhabited the area around the Caspian Sea from the tenth century B.C. and poured into southern Russia and defeated the Scythians around 200 B.C.

We have spent quite a bit of time looking at what ancient history has to say about Rosh. But what do all of these ancient names and places have to do with the current situation in the former Soviet Union?

The ancient Sarmatians were tribes of Iranian people who were known by the Assyrians as the Rashu, by the Babylonians as the Rasapu, and by the central Asians as the Rukhs-As or Rus. We know that in Ezekiel's day the Rasapu, a Sarmatian tribe, were defeated by the Babylonians in the area that today is a part of Armenia, Azerbaijan, and Georgia—three former Soviet republics. The main body of the Sarmatians, however, occupied the area east of the Caspian Sea in central Asia. This territory today is occupied by the five former central Asian republics of the U.S.S.R.

The Sarmatians in central Asia moved into the area north of the Black Sea around 200 B.C., defeated the Scythians, and began their four-hundred-year reign of the southern steppes of Russia. The Sarmatians left their imprint clearly upon this area. The Volga River in modern Russia is called the Rhos by an anonymous Greek author in a book of geography in the fifth century A.D.[32] Moreover, the Rus known to the Arab and Byzantine writers probably lived somewhere in southern Russia.

Gesenius, the Hebrew scholar, says that Rosh is "undoubtedly the Russians, who are mentioned by the Byzantine writers of the tenth century, under the name Ros, dwelling to the north of Taurus . . . as dwelling on the river Rha (Wolga)."[33]

Rus was also the name of the great Kievan Empire (A.D. 862). Eventually, the name Ros or Rus became the name of the entire area of modern Russia when the Latin suffix *ia* was added somewhere in the sixteenth century. One Russian historian even goes so far as to say, "The first reference to the . . . Russ, the ancestors of the Russian rulers, is found in Ezekiel 38:2."[34]

Rosh Today

The ancient Sarmatians, who were known as Rashu, Rasapu, Ros, and Rus, are the people Ezekiel called Rosh in Ezekiel 38:2. The Sarmatians originally inhabited the land around the Caspian Sea, which is territory inhabited by eight of the former Soviet republics—Armenia, Georgia, Azerbaijan, Kazakhstan, Kirghizia, Uzbekistan, Turkmenistan, and Tajikistan. As we saw in the last chapter, six of these former republics are Muslim nations. The only two that are not Muslim are Georgia and Armenia. The six former republics that are Islamic are beginning to form close ties with other Muslim nations around them.

The alliances foretold in Ezekiel 38–39 seem to be unfolding before our eyes! But there's more!

In the year 200 B.C. the Sarmatians invaded the southern Russian steppes into the area of modern Ukraine and Russia. Therefore, it is clear from ancient history that Rosh *is* Russia! The ancient people of Rosh inhabited the former southern republics of the U.S.S.R. and Russia. Therefore, we know that these parts of the former Soviet Union are included in the great Gog coalition in Ezekiel 38–39. The Scythians of Magog and the Sarmatians of Rosh clearly show us that *the Russians are coming!*

Many have thought that the fall of the Soviet Union totally eliminated Russia from the prophetic picture. However, the fall of the Soviet Union and the rise of the independent Muslim republics may actually give Russia a stronger alliance and stake in Islamic affairs. The *Jerusalem Post* reports:

> What the West seems to have forgotten is that Russian interest in the Middle East precedes the advent of communism. It is not about to disappear with the demise of the Soviet empire. In fact, Russia has certain advantages in the regional power play. Communism's sweet promise may have lost its appeal for the region's oppressed peoples. But the rise of independent Islamic republics within the Russian orbit may become a far more effective weapon in the battle for their hearts and minds.[35]

The *Intelligence Digest* of October 29, 1993, reports:

> Since the collapse of the Soviet Union and its empire
> in Eastern Europe we have argued that the most-
> likely first place for Russia to seek to regain its lost
> influence in world affairs is in the Middle East. The
> evidence that Moscow is developing an anti-Western
> strategy in the region is growing.

Keep your eyes on the Islamic world, but don't count
the Russians out. When Gog invades Israel, the Russians
will be there, and the present conditions in Russia make
such an invasion more likely than ever before!

FOUR

The Wounded Bear

THE well-known national symbol for Russia is the bear. When the Soviet Union dissolved, many thought that the bear would go into hibernation, but nothing could be farther from the truth. The bear is more dangerous than ever before. The most dangerous kind of bear is not a black bear, a polar bear, a kodiak bear, or even a grizzly bear. The most dangerous kind of bear is a wounded bear, a starving bear, or a mother bear robbed of her cubs. All three of these pictures describe accurately the current situation in Russia. Russia, who only three years ago ruled over a vast empire including fifteen republics, is now a struggling, poverty-stricken, crime-laden nation with a devastated economy and a humiliated national ego. Let's trace some of the developments that have made Russia a more dangerous bear than ever before.

UnBEARable Conditions

The Great Depression in the United States from 1929 to 1933 caused a drop in our standard consumer spending of 21 percent. But the standard of living in Russia in 1990 was worse than ours in 1929. Add to that the following conditions:

- A drop in consumer spending of 38 percent in 1992 alone
- A monthly inflation of 20 percent, which experts fear may soon increase to 50 percent a month
- Annual fall in output of 15 percent
- Skyrocketing unemployment
- A 15 percent decline of the ruble against the dollar last year
- Massive shortages and isolation from world markets

The terrible economic conditions in Russia are having a dramatic ripple effect throughout every aspect of life in the nation. Life in Russia is becoming more miserable in every way imaginable. However, not only is life there becoming worse but it is also becoming shorter. In 1993 the life expectancy of Russian men dropped from sixty-two to fifty-nine years—thirteen years less than their American counterparts. This represents the largest one-year decline since World War II. The *Dallas Morning News* (February 2, 1994) reports:

> "It is a spectacular decline, the largest one-year decline since the war," said Murray Feshback, research professor of demography at Georgetown Uni-

versity in Washington. "It's really unprecedented for any developed country."

Life expectancy for Russian women is also declining, though not as sharply. It fell from 73.8 years in 1992 to 73.2 last year. The current figures are now below all major industrialized countries and are fast approaching Third World levels according to Mr. Feshback. The figures quantify what many Russians already feel in their bones: Poverty, violence, disease, and stress are taking a huge toll on public health.

Within this same article, one Russian social medicine expert lists the following five causes for this dramatic fall in the average life expectancy of Russian men.

1. Free-market reforms have created a new class of wealthy entrepreneurs, but these same reforms have also impoverished many more Russians.
2. Although starvation is still rare, the average Russian's diet is worsening. The price of meat, poultry, and fresh vegetables is rising faster than wages.
3. Ecological consequences of communist-era industrial policies have polluted the health of millions of Russians. Factories in the Ural Mountains cover entire cities in soot. The Volga River, which is a major source of drinking water for many Russian cities, is full of caustic chemicals.
4. Disease is on the rise (cholera, diphtheria, whooping cough).

5. The Russian government is in no financial condition to begin cleaning up the environment or to start investing in public health care or sanitation.

In addition to the economic free fall in Russia, there is also an unparalleled increase in crime and brutish violence. The most alarming aspect of the crime wave is the rise in graft and gangsterism. The *New York Times International* (Jan. 30, 1994) reports:

> While most Russians are not surprised to hear that criminal gangs seem to be taking over the country, a top-level Government report has laid out the gangs' reach in stark terms: Organized crime has Russia by the throat, squeezing the life out of the fledgling private sector and holding the Government itself hostage.

From 1992 to 1993 murder has increased 27 percent, crimes causing serious injury are up 24 percent, and crimes committed with firearms are up an astonishing 250 percent.

Life in Russia is indeed becoming unBEARable!

The Return of the Old Guard

One dramatic result of the horrible economic conditions in Russia is that the political landscape is beginning to change. On December 12, 1993, communists, hard-liners, and nationalists won the majority of seats in Russia's powerful lower house, the Duma. However, not only has the parliament been overrun by communists and conservative hard-liners but other key government positions are being filled by the Old Guard. For instance, Ivan Rybkin, a former Communist Party official, was elected speaker of the Duma, and Victor Chernomyrdin, a hard-line conservative, is the new prime minister of Russia. Harvard economist Jeffrey Sachs, a former adviser to the Russian government, warns that the communist Old Guard has essentially retaken almost all of the major power positions. His opinion is that "they are going to pursue dangerous policies" (*Time,* "One Giant Step Backward," George M. Taber, January 31, 1994). The prospects for reversing the current trend do not look promising. According to CIA director Robert Gates, long-term prospects for reform in Russian remain "iffy."

The powerful emergence of hard-line nationalists is especially significant in light of the Russian constitution, which has created a dictatorial presidency with immense power. The president now has absolute power to declare war by himself. If a hard-liner were to ascend to the presidency in the upcoming 1996 election, the wounded bear could strike out in ferocious fury.

The current economic, political, and social scenario in Russia is ripe for a nationalistic, power-crazed leader like Gog in Ezekiel 38–39 to burst on the scene and seize control. Many experts are equating the economic, political, and social situation in Russia today with the desperate conditions that ushered Adolph Hitler to power sixty years ago.

In the 1920s Germany suffered from hyperinflation, political instability, and national humiliation as a result of her defeat in World War I. Russia has runaway inflation, political instability, and a devastated national ego resulting from the dissolution of the Soviet empire. The Russians desperately crave a leader who will rescue them from the death grip of poverty and restore their lost empire. Robert Cullen captured the current scenario in this statement: "If the people of Russia become poorer and more desperate, they will become like a cornered bear. When a bear is cornered, she rears up on her hind legs and lashes out. All the Russian people need is an ideology and a leader to direct their anger" ("Slouching toward Chaos," *Los Angeles Times*, Jan. 12, 1992).

Amazingly, a man dubbed the "Russian Hitler" is experiencing a meteoric rise in popularity and influence in Russian politics. His name is Vladimir Zhirinovsky.

DemaGOG

As recently as one year ago, the world had never heard of Vladimir Volfovich Zhirinovsky. In the last year his face has been seen around the world on television and in magazines, newspapers, and periodicals. His notorious antics have received worldwide news coverage.

The whole world seems to be asking this question: Who is Vladimir Volfovich Zhirinovsky? Who is the man whose party recently won 24 percent of the popular vote of Russia? Who is the man who is favorably postured to make a run for the presidency of Russia in 1996? Here are thirteen terrible facts about this rising star in Russia:

1. His first name is Vladimir, which means "master of the world." His middle name indicates his father was a wild canine, and his wild statements reveal an evil and ambition unknown in the animal kingdom.
2. In spite of the fact that his own father is Jewish, he is strongly anti-Semitic, blaming the Jews for the first two world wars. Concern among Jews is rising. The *New York Times International* (Feb. 6, 1994) reports: "Jews must prepare themselves for the 1996 presidential elections, when Mr. Zhirinovsky or someone else in the opposition might prevail. 'We must hope for the best but prepare for the worst.'"
3. He has uttered myriad outrageous statements and threats. He threatened World War III when Germany refused to let him visit. He recently said, "Let us make others suffer." And concerning Lithuania he said, "I'll bury radioactive waste along the Lithuanian border and put up powerful fans and blow the stuff across at night. They'll all get radiation sickness. They'll die of it. When they either die or get down on their knees, I'll stop." He also claims to have an "elipton" weapon that kills by producing a massive impulse of sound.
4. He is an ultranationalist who desires to recreate the Russian Empire and even abrogate the 1867 treaty

deeding Alaska to the United States. He wants to annex parts of Poland, Finland, and Afghanistan. The motto on his campaign posters is "I will bring Russia up off her knees." In 1991 he said, "I say it quite plainly—when I come to power, there will be a dictatorship."

5. He is being compared to Adolph Hitler. German newspapers are calling him "the new Hitler" because when he speaks, like Hitler, he is transformed and his audience is too. Like Hitler, he has a fascination with the occult. During a recent trip to Bulgaria he consulted with Baba Vanga, the most famous psychic in Bulgaria.

6. There are strong rumors circulating that he is a homosexual.

7. He is strongly supported by the Russian military. The Russian military overwhelmingly supported his party with 80 percent of the military vote in the December 12, 1993, parliamentary elections because of his vow to resurrect the Russian Empire.

8. He is considered a strong candidate for the Russian presidency in 1996. In a November 1992 poll, 29 percent of the residents of Moscow said they would vote for Zhirinovsky for president. He is capitalizing on three main issues to garner support: the military, crime, and poverty. He carefully tailors his speeches to the specific target audience. His hard line on crime, strong support for capital punishment, and promises of economic relief are winning strong support with a

citizenry in need of reassurance. According to the *New York Times International:*

> If decisive and systematic measures are not taken, and if the political will to do battle with crime is not shown soon, then the populist promises of Zhirinovsky to restore law and order could gather tens of millions of Russians (Jan. 30, 1994).

> The installation last week of a new Russian Government . . . inspired no shortage of doom-laden predictions, including: hyperinflation, a cut in living standards, a fixed ruble, price and wage controls and a general collapse that would hand the country over to someone like Vladimir V. Zhirinovsky in the 1996 presidential elections, if not sooner. Unfortunately, some of these prophecies are likely to prove true (Jan. 23, 1994).

9. He advocates Russian conquest and control of the Persian Gulf and the Mediterranean. The title of his autobiography and political manifesto is *Last Dash to the South,* in which he says:

> I yearn to see Russian soldiers wash their boots in the warm waters of the Indian Ocean and switch to year-round summer uniforms: light boots, short-sleeved fatigues without a tie, open collars and a small modern Russian submachine gun. . . . So there is only one option. We must carry out this opera-

tion, code-named "last dash to the south." . . . Our Army will perform this task. This will be a method of ensuring the survival of the nation as a whole; it will be the basis for the renaissance of the Russian Army. . . . That's not all. I simply did not want to go in for politics. I had already begun to develop my own geopolitical concept. I don't want to give it my name, the Zhirinovsky formula, say, but the last "dash" to the south and Russia's outlet to the shores of the Indian Ocean and Mediterranean Sea are really the task of saving the Russian nation. . . . The last "dash" to the south. I dream of Russian soldiers washing their boots in the warm waters of the Indian Ocean and switching to summer uniform forever. Lightweight boots, lightweight trousers, short-sleeved open-necked shirts with no tie, lightweight caps. So the idea emerged of the "last dash"—last because it will probably be the last repartition of the world. And it must be carried out in a state of shock therapy, suddenly, swiftly, and effectively. . . . This operation—the last "dash" south—is not the Barbarossa plan (Hitler's plan for the invasion of Russia), not Napoleon's plan, not the military ventures of Swedish King Charles XII. It is purely a Russian variant, it has been elaborated by Russia's very fate. Otherwise, Russia will be unable to develop and will perish. . . . So the advance to the south is nothing new for Russia. . . . Therefore Russia should go south and reach the shores of the warm Indian Ocean. This is not just my whim. It is Russia's destiny. It is fate. It is Russia's great exploit. We must do it, because we have no choice. There is no other way for us. It is geopolitics. Our development demands it. Like a child who has outgrown his clothes and must put on new ones.

10. For Zhirinovsky, the year 1994 is the key year. He says:

> I think there are still bright prospects ahead of us, and 1993 is the last year of delay, instability, uncertainty. In 1994, progress in a positive direction will begin. . . . We must accomplish this surge of ours to the south, this last southern "Dash," the Russians' last campaign, in order once and for all to put an end to the danger on the Fatherland's southern borders.

In late 1993 after the parliamentary elections, he said, "Today is the beginning of orgasm; the whole nation, I promise you will experience orgasm next year." He has said that his Liberal Democratic Party "may definitely come to power in 1994!"

11. Zhirinovsky met recently with Saddam Hussein. He often favorably mentions Hussein in his speeches, and there are continuing rumors that Hussein helped finance Zhirinovsky's political campaign. Zhirinovsky says, "They know me in Iraq as maybe the closest friend of the Iraqi people. . . . I have met personally . . . with Saddam Hussein, who, for two years after the war, received no foreigners at all, least of all Russians. . . . He received only me in November 1992. We talked for four hours in his palace at Baghdad. It was

an interesting trip. By plane to Amman, then nearly 14 hours through the desert to Baghdad. A week in Baghdad. A meeting with the country's supreme leader on Saturday 21 November. We talked for a long time; Saddam Hussein listened and asked questions."

12. Zhirinovsky was raised in Alma-Ata, Kazakhstan, which is in ancient Magog. In chapter 2 we noted that Gog is of the land of Magog, or central Asia which includes the nation of Kazakhstan. Zhirinovsky fits this prophecy like a glove.

13. In his book, Zhirinovsky sets forth his vision for the world. He envisions the world divided into four great geopolitical spheres of influence: an Eastern Power with Japan and China ruling Indonesia, Malaysia, the Philippines, and Australia; a Western Power with Europe controlling North Africa; an American Power with the United States and Canada dominating Latin and South America; and a Northern Power where Russia controls central Asia and the Middle East. This is almost the identical alignment of nations that will exist in the last days predicted in the Bible. We will consider this alignment of nations in more detail in chapter 12.

The Word of God declares that in the end times a power-crazed ruler referred to as Gog will lead a massive Russian-Islamic invasion into Israel. This man, like Zhirinovsky, will have an insatiable imperial appetite (Ezek. 38:9-12); he will be an anti-Semite with a desire to conquer and plunder Israel (Ezek. 38:8-12); he will be "of the land of Magog" (Ezek. 38:2); he will be the leader of Rosh, or Russia (Ezek. 38:2); and he will lead an ill-fated "Last Dash South" into Israel, where he and his army will be decimated on the mountains of Israel (Ezek. 38:18-22). While it is obviously much too early to know if this man is Gog of Ezekiel 38–39, he certainly has many of the characteristics that such a leader will undoubtedly possess. We should keep our eyes on this man and his movements in the days ahead. The *Jerusalem Post* (Jan. 29, 1994, p. 24) issued this powerful warning:

> The extreme nationalist alliance led by Vladimir Zhirinovsky will sooner or later take control of Russia, because there are no forces capable of counter-acting it, a political analyst from Moscow predicted last week. "Zhirinovsky is worse than Stalin or Hitler because he has nuclear power," said Sergei Grigoriantz, editor at the Glasnost information agency and a former dissident who spent more than a decade in Soviet jails and hard-labor camps. Grigoriantz is one of the founders of an antifascist group that is trying to combat the ultraright movement. He was speaking at a Hebrew University seminar on the political situation in Russia. "The West does not understand the mentality of people like Zhirinovsky and does not take his territorial ambitions seriously," Grigoriantz said. "Zhirinovsky will begin a war to gain territory, and there will be a threat to the entire civilized world."

These are the final words in Zhirinovsky's book, *Last Dash to the South*. They sound like they are straight from the pages of Ezekiel 38–39:

> Let Russia successfully accomplish its last "dash" to the south. I see Russian soldiers gathering for this last southern campaign. I see Russian commanding officers in the headquarters of Russian divisions and armies, sketching the lines of march, of troop formations, and the end points of their marches. I see planes at airbases in the southern districts of Russia. I see submarines surfacing off the shores of the Indian Ocean and landing craft approaching the shores, where soldiers of the Russian Army are already marching, infantry combat vehicles are advancing, and vast numbers of tanks are on the move. Russia is at last accomplishing its final military campaign.

FIVE

Let's Talk Turkey

G OG of the land of Magog will be the leader of this great end-time assault force on Israel. As we have seen, the land of Magog primarily includes the former southern republics of the Soviet Union that are Muslim nations. We have also seen that Gog is the prince or leader of Rosh, which is Russia. However, Gog and Magog will not act alone. Four more sons of Japheth will ally themselves with him to attack Israel in the last days. These four ancient names are Meshech, Tubal, Gomer, and Beth-togarmah. These names by themselves do not tell us very much, but when we discover where these ancient lands were located, they provide incredible insight into the present-day nations who will accompany Gog in his ill-fated invasion.

Meshech

Meshech was the sixth son of Japheth, who was one of Noah's three sons. The name Meshech occurs in the Old

Testament six times outside Ezekiel 38–39 (Gen. 10:2; 1 Chron. 1:5, 17; Ps. 120:5; Ezek. 27:13; and Ezek. 32:26). All we know about Meshech from the Old Testament is that Meshech and his partners Javan and Tubal traded with the ancient city of Tyre, exporting slaves and vessels of bronze in exchange for Tyre's merchandise. That's all the Bible tells us about ancient Meshech. However, ancient history has a great deal to say about the location and people of ancient Meshech.

The most common identification of Meshech by Bible prophecy students is the Russian city of Moscow. Many have thought that Meshech is Muskovi, the old name for Russia. The former view was popularized by the *Scofield Reference Bible* and has been so widely accepted that to even question it in some circles is considered heresy. However, the only evidence to support this conclusion is the similarity in the sound of the names—Meshech and Moscow. The similarity is even more pronounced if the Greek name for Meshech is used—Moschi. The problem is that similarity in sound or pronunciation alone is a wholly insufficient basis to equate two names.

As we noted above, the Bible tells us that ancient Meshech was a trading partner with ancient Tyre, which is located in the modern nation of Lebanon. Clearly ancient Tyre did not carry on trade with the ancient city of Moscow or any other tribes in that region. In Ezekiel 38, Ezekiel had historical places in mind that existed in his day, not modern nations. However, by carefully locating the historical places Ezekiel mentions we can determine the modern-day equivalent of these historical places.

History reveals to us that ancient Meshech should be identified with the ancient Mushki of the Assyrians and the Moschi of the classical Greek writers. The ancient Mushki or Musku are first mentioned during the twelfth century B.C. in northern Mesopotamia.[36]

In the ninth century they are mentioned in several Assyrian inscriptions as inhabiting Phrygia in northern Anatolia (modern Turkey).[37] Their king was named Mi-ta-a, which some scholars believe to be equated with the famous King Midas of Phrygia.

Much later, in the writings of Herodotus in the fifth century B.C., the Mushki are called the Moscheni and are located in the mountains southeast of the Black Sea.[38] This geographical location is in the northeastern part of the modern nation of Turkey.

Josephus, a Romanized Jewish scholar in the first century A.D., identified the descendants of Meshech as the Mosocheni who lived in ancient Cappadocia.[39] Ancient maps uniformly show that the ancient Mushki and Moschi were located in Cilicia and Cappadocia, which are in the southeastern and northeastern parts of modern Turkey, respectively.[40]

The *Brown-Driver-Briggs Hebrew—Lexicon of the Old Testament* states that in Persian times, which was approximately thirty to fifty years after Ezekiel wrote, Meshech was located near the southeast part of the Black Sea.[41]

The area southeast of the Black Sea is clearly in the modern nation of Turkey.

Tubal

The ancient name of Tubal first appears in the Bible in Genesis 10:2. Tubal was the fifth son of Japheth and the brother of Meshech. The name Tubal appears in the Old Testament five times outside Ezekiel 38–39 (Gen. 10:2; 1 Chron. 1:5; Isa. 66:19; Ezek. 27:13; and Ezek. 32:26). The generally accepted view among students of Bible prophecy has been that the name Tubal is preserved in the modern Russian city of Tobolsk. The identification of Tubal was also greatly promoted by the popularity of the *Scofield Reference Bible.* Scofield's reference note on Ezekiel 38:2 reads, "That the primary reference is to the Northern (European) powers headed by Russia, all agree. . . . The reference to Meshech and Tubal (Moscow and Tobolsk) is a clear mark of identification."[42]

Once again, as with Meshech, the identification is based on similarity of sound and pronunciation and because of the close proximity of these names to Rosh. A closer examination of ancient Tubal reveals that it was not even close to the modern city of Tobolsk in the former Soviet Union.

The first mention of ancient Tubal is in the ninth century B.C. in Assyrian inscriptions where it is called Tabal. The *Cambridge Ancient History* records that ancient Tabal is biblical Tubal.[43] Ancient Tabal was just west of ancient Meshech in eastern Anatolia, which is the modern nation of Turkey. Tubal and Meshech were closely related to one another in ancient history. They were right next to one another geographically, and in 713 B.C. they became allies against the Assyrians.[44] The classical Greek writers often linked these two nations closely together and called them the Tibareni and the Moschi. Interestingly, Tubal and Meshech are also closely related to one another in the Bible as well. They always appear together in Scripture except in Isaiah 66:19 and Psalm 120:5.

Hebrew scholars also equate Tubal with ancient Tabal and the Tibareni. The *Brown-Driver-Briggs Hebrew—Lexicon of the Old Testament* identifies Tubal as the Tubalu in east Asia Minor, or Cappadocia, which is in modern Turkey.[45] The Hebrew scholar Gesenius says that Tubal is the Tibareni, a nation in Asia Minor dwelling by the Black Sea to the west of the Moschi.[46]

The final mention of the Tibareni and Moschi was by the Greek historian Herodotus. He tells us that at the time of the Persian king Darius, which was approximately 500 B.C., both the Tibareni and Moschi inhabited the territory along the southeast shores of the Black Sea.[47] This territory today is in the modern nation of Turkey.

Therefore, at every point in the history of Meshech and Tubal, these two nations occupied territory in the modern nation of Turkey. To ascribe any other location to them is totally inconsistent with the clear facts of ancient history.

Gomer

Gomer was the first son of Japheth, the son of Noah. We have already looked at three of Gomer's brothers—Magog, Meshech, and Tubal. Outside the reference to Gomer in Ezekiel 38:6, the name is found only in Genesis 10:2-3 and 1 Chronicles 1:5-6, both of which are genealogies. Therefore, the Bible tells us nothing specific about the location of the descendants of Gomer.

The view commonly adopted by Bible prophecy students is that the descendants of Gomer eventually made their way into Europe, predominantly settling in Germany. Reference is frequently made to the Jewish Talmud where Gomer is stated to be the Germani or the Germans. This view has been almost universally accepted by prophecy students especially during the time when East Germany was closely allied to the Soviet Union. Some even include all of Eastern Europe and the Warsaw Pact nations under the umbrella of Gomer. During the time the Soviet Union dominated these nations, this view flourished. However, now that the Soviet Union has fallen and the Iron Curtain in Eastern Europe has been ripped in half, the view that Gomer is Eastern Europe no longer holds the appeal it once did.

This case serves as a clear example of why Bible prophecy should not be interpreted in light of current events, but rather current events should be interpreted in light of the Bible. The danger of interpreting Bible prophecy in light of current events was clearly highlighted during the 1930s and 1940s when Mussolini was identified as the

Antichrist and Armageddon was hailed as just around the corner. We must be careful not to sensationalize prophecy or try to force it into the mold of current events. God's Word is sensational enough by itself and doesn't need our help. However, we *are* called to understand the times in which we live and to carefully discern God's prophetic program. This brings us back to the proper identification of Gomer.

Ancient history clearly identifies biblical Gomer with the Akkadian *Gi-mir-ra-a* and the Armenian *Gamir.* The *Cambridge Ancient History* states that the Assyrian Gimirrai is the Hebrew *Gomer.*[48] However, the common designation for the descendants of Gomer in ancient times was the Cimmerians, which was derived from the Greek word *Kimmerioi.*

The Cimmerians, whose name appears in Homer's *Odyssey*, occupied the southern Russian steppe along the north shore of the Black Sea between the Don and Danube rivers since around 1200 B.C. The modern location of this area is the former Soviet republic known as the Ukraine. In the eighth century B.C. the Scythians (Magog) invaded the territory north of the Black Sea and forced the Cimmerians out of southern Russia. The Cimmerians fled to the south, crossed the Caucasus Mountains, and poured into the area of Lake Van in eastern Anatolia (modern Turkey).

In the following century the Cimmerians were pushed out of the Lake Van area by the Assyrians and moved to the west where they conquered the Phrygians and Lydians in central and western Anatolia. After taking Lydia they soon began to decline and were finally defeated around 630 B.C.

Thereafter, they are no longer mentioned in ancient historical sources, but it is commonly believed that they settled in the area of Cappadocia, which today is in central and north-central Turkey. Josephus identified the people of Galatia with Gomer. He says that the people the Greeks called the Galatians were the Gomerites.[49] The Galatians, of course, lived in an area that today is in the west-central part of Turkey.

Therefore, we know that, after their expulsion from the southern steppes of Russia in 700 B.C. until the first century A.D., the descendants of Gomer resided in the region that is in the modern nation of Turkey.

While it is true that some of the descendants of Gomer may have migrated into the region of the Balkans in modern Eastern Europe, especially Bulgaria, the ancient Gimirrai that Ezekiel knew and referred to resided in ancient Cappadocia, or modern Turkey.

Beth-togarmah

The name Togarmah appears in the Old Testament only three times outside the reference in Ezekiel 38:6 (Gen. 10:3; 1 Chron. 1:6; and Ezek. 27:14). In Genesis 10:3 we find that Togarmah was the third son of Gomer. Both references in Ezekiel are to Beth-togarmah rather than just Togarmah. The names are the same in each case; the word *Beth* at the beginning of the word is the Hebrew word for "house" or "place of." It simply means the house or place of Togarmah. The only description of ancient Togarmah is in Ezekiel 27:14 where we find that Beth-togarmah traded with ancient Tyre in horses, war horses, and mules. Horse trading was Togarmah's claim to fame. This tells us something about what the inhabitants of Togarmah did, but unlike the other descendants of Japheth mentioned in Ezekiel 38, the Bible gives us some information about the general location of Beth-togarmah.

The only indication in the Bible about Togarmah's location is the statement in Ezekiel 38:6: "Beth-togarmah *from* the remote parts of the north with all its troops." We know, therefore, that Togarmah was far north of Israel. That all the invaders with Gog will come from the remote parts of the north is repeated in Ezekiel 38:15 and 39:2. This statement has led many Bible students to identify Togarmah with the former Soviet Union because it is the nation farthest north of Israel. Togarmah is most often identified with the ancient Cossacks of southern and eastern Russia whose love for horses is renowned. However, it is incorrect to infer that because Russia is the nation farthest north of Israel, it is the one meant in the Bible.

Most Bible scholars and scholars of ancient history relate biblical Togarmah to the ancient Hittite city of Tegarma, an important city in eastern Cappadocia (modern Turkey). Togarmah was both the name of a district and a city in the border of Tubal in eastern Cappadocia. Togarmah was known variously in history as Tegarma,

Tagarma, and Takarama. The ancient Assyrians referred to this city as Til-garimmu.[50] One of the maps in the *Cambridge Ancient History* locates Til-garimmu on the northeast border of Tubal in the northeast part of modern Turkey.[51] Gesenius, the Hebrew scholar, identified Togarmah as a northern nation abounding in horses and mules, located in ancient Armenia.[52] The ancient area of Armenia is located in the modern nation of Turkey.

Brown-Driver-Briggs in their Hebrew lexicon identify Togarmah with Til-garimmu in northwest Asia Minor, or present-day Turkey.[53]

A few scholars deviate from this identification. Josephus regarded Togarmah as the Phrygians who were famous for their horses.[54] In any event, ancient Phrygia is also in modern Turkey, so his identification does little to change the final result. Others equate Togarmah with the classical Gauraena or modern Gurun, which is the same site as ancient Til-garimmu.[55] Some have placed Togarmah, as early as the fourteenth century B.C., on the important trade route between Carchemish and Harran.

But while scholars have differed slightly on the exact location of ancient Togarmah, it is always associated with a city or district within the boundaries of the modern nation of Turkey.

Yet if this identification is true, what do we do with the statement in Ezekiel 38:6 that Togarmah comes from the "remote [or remotest] parts of the north"? Doesn't this statement mean that Togarmah must come from the former Soviet Union since Russia is the farthest geographical point north of Israel? The answer to this question is no. Forcing a geographical location upon Togarmah that is totally inconsistent with the clear witness of ancient history would be grossly twisting the evidence. Moreover, modern Turkey fits the description given because it is clearly to the far north parts of the Promised Land.

Turkey Today

Having seen that Meshech, Tubal, Gomer, and Togarmah all refer to the modern nation of Turkey, now it's really time to talk Turkey. What do we know about the modern nation of Turkey? Would modern Turkey have any reason to join with other nations and invade Israel?

The language of the nation of Turkey is Turkish, and 99 percent of the population is Sunni Muslim. The population of Turkey is forty-five million. The favorite saying of the Turks is *"Biz bize benezeriz,"* which means "We resemble ourselves." However, the Turks are coming more and more to resemble their neighbors.

The modern nation of Turkey is truly a nation torn between two worlds. During the recent Persian Gulf crisis, the Turks sided with the West against Iraq and were considered a key link in the war against the Iraqis. Turkey desires to have strong ties with the West mainly for economic reasons. Traditionally, the Turks have not felt a special kinship with either the Arabs or the Persians (Iranians). They have mainly been drawn to their neighbors for economic reasons.

All this has begun to change with the independence of

the five Muslim republics of the former Soviet Union. The names of these five former republics are Kazakhstan, Uzbekistan, Kirghizia, Turkmenistan, and Tajikistan. While Turkey has clearly been drawn to these former Soviet republics for economic reasons, Turkey also shares strong linguistic and ethnic ties with these nations. All of these nations speak Turkic languages with the exception of Tajikistan, where the language is similar to Iranian Farsi.

Turkey views itself as the bridge between the West and the new Muslim states of the former Soviet Union. In a recent article in *Time* entitled "The Phoenix of Turkish Politics," the new Turkish prime minister, Suleiman Demirel, is quoted as saying:

> Turkey's position is more important than before. A new window of opportunity has opened for us with the Turkic republics. They speak our language. We are urging them to remain secular and to switch to the Latin alphabet. We are trying to revitalize a Black Sea economic union to include both the Balkans and the new Turkic republics.[56]

An article in *U.S. News and World Report* highlights Turkey's interest in central Asian nations.

> Turkey is trying to carve out a new identity as the economic, cultural, and linguistic center of gravity that tugs this new frontier toward the West. In the process, it seeks to create a new "Turkic" world. . . .

"It is Atlantis rediscovered," enthuses Gengis Chandar, a columnist with the Turkish newspaper *Sabah.*

No one is exploiting the Turkish connection more enthusiastically than Turkey's neofascist right wing, with the Turkish government's tacit collusion. Prime Minister Demirel is flirting with Alpaslan Turkes, a former Turkish army colonel who helped engineer the overthrow of Turkey's elected government in 1960 and who now heads the right-wing Nationalist Labor Party in parliament. . . . "We would like Turkey to organize, operate, and coordinate among all Turkic groups in the world," he told *U.S. News.*[57]

Turkey is clearly wooing these former Soviet republics. Turkey recently offered ten thousand scholarships to the young men of these Muslim states to come to Turkey and study business, and will give the region $1.1 billion in agricultural credits and investment guarantees. Turkey also opened embassies in all of the new central Asian nations in the spring of 1992.

Part of Turkey's interest is focused on the vast mineral wealth of the five former Soviet republics in central Asia. These republics are rich in gold, silver, uranium, oil, coal, and natural gas.

Turkey is also witnessing a rise in fundamentalist Islam within its borders. Does modern Turkey, the land of ancient Meshech, Tubal, Gomer, and Beth-togarmah, have anything in common with ancient Magog and Rosh, the former southern Soviet republics and Russia? The answer is clearly yes! Turkey has economic, linguistic, religious, political, and emotional ties to the newly independent Muslim republics, and these ties are becoming stronger and more obvious as these words are being written.

Conclusion

Three of the invaders in Ezekiel 38–39 have now been identified: the former southern Soviet republics, Russia, and Turkey. The former southern Soviet republics and Turkey have almost everything in common—language, religion, political ties, economic compatibility, and, of course, a common Muslim hatred of Israel. It's not too difficult to imagine these two getting together in the near future to invade Israel.

But before we consider what may be the current setting of the stage for this event, we have a few more nations to add before the picture is complete! Let us move on to the final four nations of the Ezekiel 38–39 coalition.

SIX

Muslims, Muslims, and More Muslims

THE prophecy of Ezekiel 38 would be amazing if we stopped right where we are in identifying the participants in this invasion. However, Ezekiel goes on in verse 5 to identify three more Muslim nations that will participate in the coalition of nations that will invade Israel in the last days: "Persia, Ethiopia, and Put with them, all of them *with* shield and helmet." These three nations, like the first three, have startling ties to one another and with the nations we have already identified. The coalition of nations in Ezekiel could be forming before our eyes! Let's look at these ancient names to identify the modern nations they represent.

Placing the Persians

The fourth ally of Gog is called simply Persia. This is the easiest of the nations in Ezekiel 38 to locate. Persia was the empire that followed the Babylonian Empire. In the second chapter of Daniel, the prophet Daniel interpreted Nebuchadnezzar's great dream of the metallic man. The five parts of the image were the head of gold, the arms and chest of silver, the belly and thighs of brass, the legs of iron, and the feet partly of iron and partly of clay. These parts of the image represent the five great Gentile world empires: Babylon, Medo-Persia, Greece, Rome, and Reunited Rome in the last days.

This same picture is given in the seventh chapter of Daniel in the form of four dreadful beasts. The first was like a lion with two wings on its back; the second was like a bear; the third was like a leopard, but the leopard had four heads and four wings on its back; and the fourth beast had seven heads and ten horns. These beasts represent the same Gentile world empires.

In the eighth chapter of Daniel, the empire that succeeded Babylon is pictured as a ram with two horns. This ram depicts the Medo-Persian Empire, according to Daniel 8:20: "The ram which you saw with the two horns represents the kings of Media and Persia."

At the time of Ezekiel's prophecy, approximately 585 B.C., Persia was still a small client kingdom under the more powerful Median king Astyges. Persia only held about fifty thousand square miles of territory. However, the Persians even in Ezekiel's time were significant enough to mention as selling their services as mercenaries to other nations (Ezek. 27:10).

Media was a major power as early as 612 B.C. when they helped Nebuchadnezzar defeat Assyria and conquer its capital city, Nineveh. The domination of the Medes continued until the rise of Cyrus II thirty-five years later, who brought the Persians to ascendancy. Cyrus defeated the surrounding nations with surprising ease, and after consolidating Media and Persia, he moved across northern Mesopotamia to Asia Minor almost unopposed. In Asia Minor he crushed a wealthy king named Croessus and then marched back east to Babylon, which he took without a battle on Saturday night, October 12, 539 B.C. The remarkable fall of Babylon is recorded in the fifth chapter of Daniel. The rise of Cyrus the Persian is one of the most amazing events in the Bible because the prophet Isaiah called Cyrus the Persian by name and described the extent and ease of Cyrus's conquerings over one hundred years before he was even born:

> "*It is I* who says of Cyrus, '*He is* My Shepherd! And He will perform all My desire.' And he declares of Jerusalem, 'She will be built,' And of the temple, 'Your foundation will be laid.'" Thus says the LORD to Cyrus His anointed, Whom I have taken by the right hand, To subdue nations before him, And to loose the loins of kings; To open doors before him so that gates will not be shut: "I will go before you and make the rough places smooth; I will shatter the doors of bronze, and cut through their iron bars. And I will give you the treasures of darkness, And hidden wealth of secret places, In order that you may know that it is I, The LORD, the God of Israel, who calls you by your name" (Isa. 44:28–45:3).

The ancient Persian Empire ruled the world from 539 B.C. until it was conquered by Alexander the Great in 334–331 B.C. Thus the great empire pictured as the arms and chest of silver in Daniel 2 and a great bear in Daniel 7 went the way of all human empires—it ended in dissolution and destruction.

Ezekiel says, however, that Persia was not finished in 331 B.C. because she will join in the Gog invasion in the last days, so it is important to identify the modern counterpart to ancient Persia. On this point there is universal agreement—the modern nation of Iran is ancient Persia. The name Persia, which was written all over the pages of ancient history, was changed to Iran in foreign usage in March 1935. Therefore, according to the thirty-eighth chapter of Ezekiel, the Iranians will join forces with Turkey, the former southern Soviet republics, and Russia to attack Israel in the last days.

Iran Today

This addition to the coalition is no surprise today. Ever since the revolution and overthrow of the Shah in 1979, the nation of Iran has been one of the world's greatest troublemakers. The Iranians are Shiite Muslims and contain the most radical branch of Islam in the world. The hatred by Iran of Israel is so obvious it requires no comment. In June 1992 Iran was asked by Lebanon to rein in Hezbollah guerrillas in southern Lebanon. The Iranians responded by refusing and saying that Iran would use all of its power to back their war on the Jewish state.

Iran also made headlines in May 1992 with the shocking news that they had obtained at least two nuclear warheads. Even more fascinating is the source of these warheads. They came from Kazakhstan, one of the former Muslim republics of the Soviet Union. The weekly Arabic magazine *Al-Watan Al-Arabi* reported in December 1991 that Iran took advantage of the crumbling of the Soviet Union to buy components for three nuclear weapons for between $130 million and $150 million. The magazine also reported that Iran has hired fifty Soviet nuclear experts to assemble them.

Iran is also engaged in a massive buildup of conventional weapons. An article entitled "The Russia-Iran Connection" in the May 30, 1992, issue of the *Jerusalem Post* says:

> What is known about Iran's conventional arming is almost as worrisome. Tehran is spending, according to Gates, at least $2 billion a year on arms. It is modernizing its navy, air force, and army. It has acquired Russian submarines, and it has sent submarine crews for training in a Russian naval base. In the hope of acquiring state-of-the-art weapons at bargain basement prices, Iran has established close contacts with the Muslim republics of the former Soviet Union.[58]

The goal of Iran is clear—they want to control the entire Middle East and spread the fundamentalist Islamic gospel. The January 25, 1993, edition of *Newsweek* reported:

> "Tehran has become the Moscow for the Muslim world," says Assad Homayoun, a former Iranian diplomat. "Iran wants to become the power in the region that promotes fundamentalism and terrorism."

In November 1991 Iran's prime minister, Hashamir Rafsanjani, assembled a council of his high command and made this bold announcement: "The objective is to eliminate the West from the Middle East and to liberate Jerusalem."[59]

On May 21, 1992, the *Jerusalem Post* stated:

> Iran clearly intends to achieve hegemony in the region and in the Islamic world, and it hopes to do so by emulating the Soviet Union in its heyday; by combining massive arming with the spreading of its fundamentalist gospel.[60]

The announced "grand design" of Iran under Rafsanjani is to unite the Muslim world into an Islamic crescent extending all the way from Indonesia in the Pacific to Mauritania in northwest Africa. This crescent would join together two billion Muslims into a tremendous military-political power! As we have already seen, Kazakhstan and the other former central Asian Soviet republics will also participate in the invasion described in

Ezekiel 38–39. Iran is already beginning to develop close ties with these former republics. The official language of the former republic of Tajikistan is very similar to the Farsi language spoken in Iran. All six of the largely Muslim states of the old Soviet Union are being wooed by both the Turks and the Iranians.

The *Intelligence Digest* of October 29, 1993, states:

> The Persian Gulf provides the closest ocean ports to Central Asia, and already two routes from the region, running through Turkmenistan and Iran, are open. A third is due to be completed next month. The first railway linking Iran with Central Asia is being built, and it is expected to be finished in late 1995.
>
> Iran and Turkmenistan are also discussing plans to lay a gas pipeline under the Caspian Sea which will then pass through Iran and Turkey to Europe.
>
> During Rafsanjani's visit, Turkmenistan's President Saparmurat Niyazov left no doubt in observers' minds of his desire to please Iran. Apart from signing nine commercial agreements, symbolic gestures of goodwill included naming a town after Rafsanjani, laying the foundation stone of "Rafsanjani Mosque," and naming a street in the capital, Ashgabat, "Tehran Street."

Interestingly, Turkey, Iran, and these new Muslim nations will all participate in the great coalition that invades Israel in the last days.

One of Iran's allies in her new quest for power is an old friend—Russia. Iran is now the beneficiary of a military assistance treaty with Russia. As a result of her alliance with Russia, Iran recently purchased a Kilo-class submarine and twenty to thirty Russian MiG-29 fighters and SU-24 bombers. Iran and Rosh are now allies just as Ezekiel predicted twenty-six hundred years ago!

With all of the alliances between Iran, the Sudan, Russia, and central Asia, we can clearly see how this coalition could be formed in the next few years or even months. The pieces are beginning to fall into place! But before we say any more about Iran, a few more key pieces need to be added.

The Kingdom of Kush

The next nation mentioned in Ezekiel 38:5 is Ethiopia, or literally Cush (see NASB footnote). Cush is mentioned in Genesis 10:6 as the first son of Ham, one of Noah's three sons. Cush was the father of Nimrod. The descendants of Ham migrated southward after the Flood and primarily constituted the nations southward of the land of Canaan. The specific identification of Cush is not nearly as easy as Persia.

There are two regions in the Old Testament referred to as Cush. The earliest references to Cush describe a land in western Mesopotamia, or the modern land of Iraq. This location is derived from the mention in Genesis 2:13 of one of the rivers that flowed out of the Garden of Eden as the river Gihon: "And the name of the second

river is Gihon; it flows around the whole land of Cush."
Some believe that Nimrod, the son of Cush, led a migra-
tion of Cushites to dominate and leave their name on the
Kassites (Cushites) who were the predecessors of the
ancient Babylonians in modern Iraq.[61] Also notice that
most of the descendants of Cush in Genesis 10:6-7 seem
to be located at the beginning in Arabia.

While it is true that the Kassites were identified with
Cush, later in the Old Testament the name Cush uniformly refers to a land in modern Africa. The problem is
specifically locating Cush in Africa. The most common
geographical location of Cush by students of Bible prophecy has been ancient Abyssinia, or modern Ethiopia.
Many Bible translations translate the ancient name Cush
as Ethiopia. The correct location, however, is the modern
nation of Sudan, which is just south of Egypt.

Ancient Cush was called *Kusu* by the Assyrians and
Babylonians, *Kos* or *Kas* by the Egyptians, and *Nubia* by
the Greeks.[62] Secular history locates Cush as the land
directly south of ancient Egypt extending down past the
modern city of Khartoum, which is the capital of the
modern nation of Sudan.[63] Bible dictionaries also identify
Cush as the region south of Egypt, namely ancient
Nubia, or modern Sudan.[64]

Hebrew scholars also locate Cush in the area south of
Egypt. The *Brown-Driver-Briggs Hebrew—Lexicon of the
Old Testament* says that Cush is the "land and people of
southern Nile valley, or Upper Egypt."[65] Gesenius doesn't
identify Cush precisely but says that all the nations that

77

came from Cush became inhabitants of Africa who are described in the Bible as very rich. He says there is no reason to place the descendants of Cush anywhere other than Africa.[66]

The article on Kush in the *Theological Wordbook of the Old Testament* says, "Kush refers to the region immediately south and east of Egypt, including modern Nubia, the Sudan, and the Ethiopia of classical writers (not modern Abyssinia)."[67]

This location is also clearly substantiated by the Old Testament. The proper name Cush is used thirty times in the Old Testament, and other than the few references mentioned above that describe a people with the name Cush in Mesopotamia, the Bible locates Cush just south of Egypt. Cush is frequently associated with its northern neighbor Egypt (Ps. 68:31; Isa. 11:11; 20:3; 45:14; Ezek. 30:4-5, 9; Dan. 11:43; Amos 9:7; Nah. 3:9). Isaiah describes Cush as lower Egypt (11:11; the word *pathros* refers to those who dwell in southern Egypt) and as being located along the Nile River (Isa. 18:1; Zeph. 3:10). The southern border of Egypt is the northern border of ancient Cush (Ezek. 29:10; Esther 1:1). The people of Cush are pictured as tall, very rich, smooth skinned, and aggressive warriors.

So what conclusion can we derive from this information? The clear evidence is that the ancient nation of Cush is the modern nation of Sudan, which is just south of Egypt as described in ancient history and the Bible. This immediately leads to the question: How could modern Sudan possibly fit into the coalition of Gog in the invasion of Israel? Isn't the Sudan a nation where there are always famines and military coups? How could they possibly become involved in an invasion like the one described in Ezekiel 38–39?

Color Sudan Green

Most people today don't realize that the modern nation of Sudan is one of only three Muslim nations in the world with a militant Islamic government. The other two are Iran and Pakistan. Sudan has been described recently as "a police state, with God."[68] The Sudan was one of the few nations who supported Iraq in the recent Persian Gulf Crisis.

In the Sudan, 75 percent of the people are Sunni Muslims, and the official language of the Sudan is Arabic, with over 50 percent of the population speaking this language. The Sudan is the largest nation in territory on the African continent and has a population of 26 million. The total area of the country is one-fourth the size of the continental United States.

The leader of the Sudan is Omar Hassan al-Bashir, who took control by means of a military coup in 1989. However, by 1990 Hassan al-Turabi, chief of the National Islamic Front, had emerged as the real leader of the regime. Turabi is a militant Muslim, and his goal is to turn the Sudan into a militant Islamic state. Turabi has vowed to spread Islam across Africa and the Middle East, beginning with his home country of Sudan.

In an article in the *New York Times Magazine,* Judith
Miller says:

> Turabi, a veteran politician who had served in
> numerous governments, was now finally in a posi-
> tion to accomplish his lifelong goal: to turn the
> Sudan into an Islamic state that would inspire mili-
> tant Islamic groups throughout the world.[69]

Turabi also said:

> Islam is become temporal. You in the West had bet-
> ter get used to it, and you should not be afraid of it.
> We are not your enemies. Besides, objectively, the
> future is ours.[70]

The total control of Islam in Sudan is shocking. Society is being recast into the mold of Iranian Islamic funda-
mentalism. In 1990 shopkeepers in Khartoum, the
capital of the Sudan, and another city named Omdurman
were required to paint their storefronts a particular color
of "Islamic Green" as part of a beautification project.
Green is the traditional color of Islam.[71]

The government has also purged the judiciary, security
forces, police, academia, banking, and business of anyone
who is not an avowed Muslim and filled key posts with
National Islamic Front sympathizers.

Michael Georgy, a freelance journalist based in Cairo,
Egypt, reports that:

Government vehicles, equipped with loudspeakers, travel through the camps and slums offering support for those who embrace Islam. . . . Students can no longer enter universities unless they pass exams in Arabic and Islam. Even in Christian primary schools, children are forced to study the Koran. . . . Coupled with the Islamization of the country is a mandatory one-month indoctrination course for students and government employees that places a heavy emphasis on Islamic teachings.[72]

The militant government in Sudan has formed an eighty-five-thousand-member militia modeled after Iran's Revolutionary Guards. Turabi has also created "Popular Defense Forces," which are paramilitary police groups composed of students and civil servants. Members of these forces are given two months of basic military training and religious indoctrination. Most neighborhoods in Sudan have "popular committees," which are cell groups headed by members of the National Islamic Front. One of the duties of the members of these groups is to report un-Islamic behavior.

Another target of the militant regime in Sudan has been the legal system. A new criminal code has been enacted based on Islamic law, or *sharia*. The code includes corporal punishments like amputations for repeated theft, stoning for adultery, lashings for other offenses, and even crucifixion. One of the most interesting additions to the criminal code is a provision for the death penalty for apostasy, or turning away from the Islamic faith.

Perhaps the most startling recent development is the new alliance between the Sudan and Iran. A *Newsweek* article entitled "A New Alliance for Terror" says:

> According to Western diplomats, Iran has also delivered light arms and ammunition, as well as some artillery, tanks, and trucks, to Sudan. . . . Other diplomats suspect the country is sponsoring training camps for radical Palestinians and Islamic militants who have been squeezed out of Libya or Syrian-controlled Lebanon.[73]

Judith Miller, in the *New York Times Magazine*, says:

> What worries some Arab analysts far more are the growing peaceful ties between Iran, a Shiite Muslim state, and Sunni Muslim Sudan—a development that reflects the closing of a historic rift between Shiite and Sunni Islamic forces—and Turabi's open attempt to fuse the formerly secular Arab nationalist movement with Islamic militancy. "If the changes we've made here take hold, it'll amount to a veritable revolution," says Turabi.[74]

Iran is believed to have concluded a twenty-five-year pact with Sudan that gives Iran access to Port Sudan, an army base in the Gebait Hills on the Red Sea. This agreement also gives Iran access to four guerilla training bases to the north of Khartoum and forward storage facilities for war material.

This is exactly what Ezekiel predicted twenty-six hundred years ago! He stated that Persia and Cush will be allies together with many other nations in the great end-time invasion of Israel! This unholy alliance is being fulfilled right before our eyes!

Clearly, militant Islam has taken control in Sudan. This fact provides a clear reason and motivation for Sudan to join forces with Iran, Turkey, and the former central Asian republics of the U.S.S.R. They are all Muslim nations who hate Israel and would jump at the chance to devour her for their own gain. The pieces of the coalition in Ezekiel 38 could be coming together!

Where Do We Put "Put"?

The final ally of Gog mentioned in Ezekiel 38 is called Put or Phut. Like Cush, Put was a son of Ham, Noah's second son (Gen. 10:6). The name Put occurs in the Old Testament six times outside Ezekiel 38. The general geographical location of Put has been disputed; however, the best evidence shows that Put was a nation located on the African continent. The vast majority of scholars place ancient Put in Africa. Gesenius says that Put was an African nation.[75] Brown-Driver-Briggs identify Put with Africa.[76]

The Bible also has quite a bit to say about Put and its general location. Isaiah placed Put between Tarshish and

Lud (Lydia) as nations that will one day hear of the glory of the Lord (Isa. 66:19).

Jeremiah lists Put between Ethiopia and Lud as a nation whose warriors would be used to aid Nebuchadnezzar in his conquest of Egypt (Jer. 46:9). Jeremiah also describes them with Cush as shield bearers, or those who can handle the shield.

Ezekiel refers to Put and his armies, along with Persia and Lud, as mercenaries of Tyre and states that these armies contributed to Tyre's splendor (Ezek. 27:10). In Ezekiel 30:5 Put is included with Egypt, Cush, Lud, Arabia, and Ethiopia as nations that will fall by the sword.

In Nahum 3:9 Put is listed with Lubim and Ethiopia as providing mercenaries in the defense of Egypt.

While none of these passages give us sufficient information to locate Put specifically, the fact that Put is repeatedly linked with African nations leads to the assumption that Put was also located in the same area.

Having found that ancient Put is located somewhere in Africa, we now need to pinpoint the precise location. In recent times some scholars have attempted to identify Put with ancient Punt, which is mentioned in Egyptian inscriptions. The area of Punt is in east Africa in the area of Somalia and extends across to Yemen on the southern end of the Arabian peninsula.

While this interpretation is possible, the most common specific location for ancient Put is Libya. This identification is based on the clear testimony of ancient history. An ancient Babylonian inscription records that Nebuchadnezzar did battle with Egypt in his thirty-seventh year and penetrated as far as Puta. The direction of Nebuchadnezzar's penetration would have been from the east of Egypt, so this would suggest that Put was the western neighbor of Egypt, or modern Libya.[77]

An ancient Persian inscription mentions Putaya as being among the tributary countries.[78] Ancient Putaya is generally identified with the modern nation of Libya. Josephus says that Put was the founder of Libya, whose inhabitants were referred to as Putites. Both Gesenius and Brown-Driver-Briggs identify Put with the African nation of Libya.

The Septuagint, which is a Greek translation of the Old Testament, renders the word *Put* as *Libues*. In light of this strong evidence, we can be quite certain that the nation that Ezekiel called Put is the modern nation of Libya.

Libya Today

Libya is no stranger in the news today. It takes no great imagination to conceive that Libya would join with the other nations in Ezekiel 38 to attack Israel. Arabic is the official language of Libya, and the official religion is Islam. Almost the entire population is Muslim and most belong to the Sunni branch of Islam. Ever since the rise of Colonel Mu'ammar al-Gadhafi to power in 1969, the nation of Libya has been a constant source of trouble and terrorism for both the West and Israel. Libya would certainly jump at the chance to join forces with the Sudan,

Iran, Turkey, and the former Muslim republics of the Soviet Union to crush the Jewish state.

Conclusion

We have now come to the end of God's Top Ten Most Wanted List in Ezekiel 38:2-6. I hope the picture is coming into focus for you! All of the nations we have seen in Ezekiel 38 are on the scene, are beginning to develop ties with one another, and are vehement, inveterate enemies of the nation of Israel. However, there is one more nation, not mentioned in Ezekiel 38, that must be added to the list. This nation will be the leader of the North African coalition that includes Sudan and Libya. Let's look now at the final participant in the great Gog confederacy, the actor that is referred to as the "king of the south."

SEVEN

Pyramid Power

THE ten names in Ezekiel 38:2-6 have all been considered, but at least one more invader will be included in the great Gog invasion. You are probably wondering why a nation not mentioned in Ezekiel would be included in this coalition, but remember, Ezekiel refers several times to "many peoples with you" (Ezek. 38:6, 9, 15, 22). This statement is probably made to convey the idea that Ezekiel has not given an exhaustive list of the allies. Hal Lindsey says:

> Ezekiel indicates that he hasn't given a complete list of allies. Enough is given, however, to make this writer amazed by the number of people and nations which will be involved.[79]

You will notice that the nations Ezekiel does list are the farthest nations in each direction known in his day:

the farthest north—Turkey, central Asia, and southern Russia; the farthest south—Sudan; the farthest east—Iran; and the farthest west—Libya. Ezekiel specifically listed these "far nations" but left the door open to include other nations closer to Israel in every direction. Therefore, it is very likely that other nations besides the ones Ezekiel specifically lists will be included in this great coalition, and one of these is Egypt.

The King of the South

Not many years after the prophet Ezekiel wrote the words in Ezekiel 38–39, another Jewish prophet, Daniel, wrote the great prophecy in Daniel 11:40-45. In that passage Daniel refers to an end-time invasion of Israel by two great powers, the king of the south and the king of the north. In the context of the passage, each of these titles refers to a coalition of nations.

Scholars generally agree that the king of the south is Egypt. This view harmonizes very well with the entire context of Daniel 11:5-35 where the Ptolemies are referred to by this designation. The Ptolemies ruled from Egypt during the fragmented period of the Greek Empire. The identification of the king of the south with Egypt is unavoidable in light of the specific reference to Egypt in 11:42-43. However, Egypt clearly does not act alone because Libya and Sudan are mentioned in conjunction with her.

Notice that the nations Egypt is allied with are Sudan and Libya, two of the nations involved in the invasion of

Ezekiel 38–39. If these passages are describing the same invasion, then Egypt will clearly be a key player in this invasion.

Ezekiel and Daniel

Ezekiel 38–39 and Daniel 11:40-45 are parallel to one another with each supplying details that the other one omits. There are several factors that prove that these two passages are describing the same basic scenario from two different vantage points. First, in both Ezekiel 38–39 and Daniel 11:40 there is an invader from the north. Daniel refers to the "king of the North," and Ezekiel says that the end-time invader will come from "the remotest parts of the north."

Second, in both of these passages, the northern invader is allied with a southern bloc of nations. In Ezekiel 38 the northern king allies himself with Cush and Put, or Sudan and Libya. In Daniel 11:43, Sudan and Libya are listed as part of the southern coalition of nations that invade Israel.

Third, the general time period of both of these passages is identified as "the latter days," or Tribulation period (Dan. 10:14; Ezek. 38:8, 16). A closer examination reveals that the specific time period in both passages is the first half of the Tribulation period when Israel is at peace. Clearly, these passages must be describing the same invasion because two invasions of this magnitude could not occur in such a short period of time in the same general area.

Fourth, prophets who were contemporaries frequently developed similar or identical themes in their writings. Ezekiel and Daniel were contemporaries, and both describe an invasion of Israel in the last days by a confederation of northern and southern forces. Moreover, both focus on the northern invader. This identical invasion prophesied by contemporary prophets is strong evidence that these two invaders are to be equated with one another.

Since Ezekiel 38–39 is describing the same events as Daniel 11:40-45 and Daniel includes Egypt as part of the southern invading force, Egypt must be included in the coalition of nations that Gog will lead into Israel to meet their doom. But how does Egypt fit into the overall picture? What interest would Egypt have in attacking Israel with other Muslim nations?

Enter the Egyptians

Egypt today is clearly not nearly as militant as Sudan or Iran. Egypt has been the only Arab nation to develop or even attempt to develop peaceful coexistence with Israel. Egypt has been the closest thing to a friend the Israelis could ever hope for in the Middle East. But all of this seems to be changing.

The Egyptian government has attempted to contain Islamic militancy through repression, co-optation, and gradual liberalization. So far the plan is working satisfactorily, but the seeds of militant Islam are still fermenting beneath the surface. Of the forty thousand mosques in

Egypt, the government only controls twenty thousand.[80] Militant factions are free to operate in about half of the mosques in Egypt, spreading their gospel of fanaticism. Experts agree that if Egypt were to fall into the hands of Muslim extremists, the balance of power in the entire region would dramatically shift. Egypt is the Arab world's most populous country and the recipient of $2.2 billion of U.S. military and economic aid each year. According to *Newsweek* of August 30, 1993:

> A growing Islamic movement there would be disastrous for Washington. Egypt is still the only Arab country to make peace with Israel, and it's the cornerstone of U.S. policy in the oil-rich Middle East. If Egypt, the most populous country in the Arab world, were to fall into the hands of militant Islamists, the political psychology of the whole region would be transformed. Certainly the radical Islamic states of Iran and Sudan would like to see Egypt join their ranks. Washington added Sudan to its list of states that sponsor terrorism, and a State Department official insisted, "Sudan is the biggest foreign patron of terrorist activities in Egypt."

Iran's intentions are clearly to use strategically situated Sudan as a launching pad for terror into Africa, the Middle East, and ultimately Israel!

God's Word tells us that Egypt will be part of the Gog invasion in the last days. While Egypt does not seem to be as radical as the other nations we have considered, remember they are Muslim and still hate Israel. Make no mistake: When the Muslim world comes together in the Tribulation to invade Israel, the Egyptians will be there!

Conclusion

All the players in the Gog coalition have now been identified. They are all taking their places on the stage and getting ready to play their parts. We know who they are and we see them coming together. The players are getting ready! It is now time to consider the events of this invasion.

Hooks in the Jaws

NOW that we know the identity of the participants we can focus on answering the "what" question. What will happen during the great Gog invasion? God has not only told us who will be involved but has also given us an amazing overview of the events that commence and consummate this intrusion into the land of Israel in the last days.

God himself revealed the events of these chapters to Ezekiel; therefore, the information is absolutely trustworthy. God says in Amos 3:7, "Surely the LORD God does nothing Unless He reveals His secret counsel To His servants the prophets." Ezekiel 38–39 is divided into seven great parts, each beginning with the words "Thus says the Lord GOD" (38:3, 10, 14, 17; 39:1, 17, 25). Ezekiel 39:8 says, "'Behold, it is coming and it shall be done,' declares the Lord GOD. 'That is the day of which I have

spoken.'" The precise fulfillment of every word in Ezekiel 38–39 is assured.

Let's look at Ezekiel 38 to see the preconditions that
lead up to this invasion, the purpose of this invasion, and
the unseen forces behind the scenes that bring it to pass.

Israel Regathered

The events in Ezekiel 38–39 presuppose the regathering
of the nation of Israel into the land. Ezekiel 38:8, 11-12
says:

> After many days you will be summoned; in the latter
> years you will come into the land that is restored
> from the sword, *whose inhabitants* have been gath-
> ered from many nations to the mountains of Israel
> which had been a continual waste; but its people
> were brought out from the nations, and they are liv-
> ing securely, all of them. . . . And you will say, "I will
> go up against the land of unwalled villages. I will go
> against those who are at rest, that live securely, all of
> them living without walls, and having no bars or
> gates; to capture spoil and to seize plunder, to turn
> your hand against the waste places which are *now*
> inhabited, and against the people who are gathered
> from the nations, who have acquired cattle and
> goods, who live at the center of the world."

Gog and his allies will attack "the mountains of
Israel," which have been repopulated by its scattered
people "brought out from the nations." The previous

chapter, Ezekiel 37, discusses the reunion of Judah and
Israel and their regathering and restoration into the land.

Ezekiel 37 is the famous vision of the valley of the dry
bones. God showed Ezekiel a vision of a valley full of dry
bones, and then God made the dry bones come to life
again. God told Ezekiel that the dry bones represented
the nation of Israel:

> Then He said to me, "Son of man, these bones are
> the whole house of Israel; behold, they say, 'Our
> bones are dried up, and our hope has perished. We
> are completely cut off.' Therefore prophesy, and say
> to them, 'Thus says the Lord GOD, "Behold, I will
> open your graves and cause you to come up out of
> your graves, My people; and I will bring you into
> the land of Israel."'" (Ezek. 37:11-12).

The fulfillment of this great passage commenced in
1948 when the Jewish state was born, continues through
the Tribulation period, and culminates at the second coming of Christ.

The regathering that began in 1948 was a regathering
in unbelief, and that is still the condition of the vast
majority of the Jews in Israel today. In Ezekiel's dry bones
vision, the first stage of the restoration of Israel is
described in 37:8: "And I looked, and behold, sinews
were on them, and flesh grew, and skin covered them;
but there was no breath in them." This has been Israel's
condition from 1948 until today, and it will continue

until Christ returns. There is no spiritual life in them! However, when Christ returns, God will breathe life into the lifeless people, and their restoration will be complete.

Israel Resting

Another precondition for the invasion of Israel in Ezekiel 38–39 is the "security" of Israel in the land. Ezekiel describes the people of Israel as "living securely" three times (38:8, 11, 14). He also says that they will be "at rest . . . all of them living without walls, and having no bars or gates" (38:11).

Obviously, this is not the present state of the nation of Israel. Israel is the most militarily alert nation in the world. However, the Bible tells us that at some time in Israel's future the nation will be secure and at rest. What events could possibly lead to this scenario in Israel? The answer is in Daniel 9:27 and Revelation 6:2-4.

Daniel 9:27 tells us that the event that signals the beginning of the seven-year Tribulation period is the making of a seven-year covenant between the Antichrist and the nation of Israel. The Antichrist will break his covenant with Israel in the middle of that period, but the first three and a half years will provide the environment for the conditions in Ezekiel 38. "And he will make a firm covenant with the many for one week, but in the middle of the week he will put a stop to sacrifice and grain offering" (Dan. 9:27).

The clear implication of this verse is that for the first half of the Tribulation the Jews will in fact live in security and offer temple sacrifices to God. The Antichrist will negotiate peace in the Middle East, and the Jews will live with a sense of security, albeit false security.

The same picture is presented in Revelation 6:2-4 in the first two seal judgments:

> And I looked, and behold, a white horse, and he who sat on it had a bow; and a crown was given to him; and he went out conquering, and to conquer. And when He broke the second seal, I heard the second living creature saying, "Come." And another, a red horse, went out; and to him who sat on it, it was granted to take peace from the earth, and that *men* should slay one another; and a great sword was given to him.

The rider on the white horse is the Antichrist. He goes out with a bow but interestingly with no arrows. His conquering is political conquering, not military. It is the rider on the red horse who comes to take peace from the earth. The clear implication is that the rider on the white horse was the agent of this peace that is now being removed by the rider on the red horse.

The Antichrist will appear on the scene as the greatest politician and problem solver the world has ever known. He will bring relative peace to the earth and to Israel, but it will be a false peace. The rider on the red horse who breaks this peace is none other than Gog and his great horde!

Amazingly, the picture of Israel at rest in Ezekiel 38 is more likely today than at any time since 1948. The world watched in astonishment and disbelief on Monday, September 13, 1993, as Yitzhak Rabin and Yasser Arafat signed their peace pact on the White House lawn in Washington, D.C. While this treaty is clearly not the seven-year covenant in Daniel 9:27, it is undoubtedly a precursor to it. Some have even referred to Yasser Arafat as "the Antichrist's John the Baptist," that is, his forerunner.

If the Antichrist were to appear on the world political scene in the next year, he would find a ready and willing ally in Israel to negotiate peace in the Middle East and enter into a covenant with him. Israel was regathered in 1948, and a resting Israel could be a reality in the very near future. When this final precondition is met, Gog will be ready to strike and eliminate his hated enemy.

Gog's Evil Plan

While Israel is resting securely in the land and enjoying peace and tranquillity from her covenant with the Antichrist, Russia and the Muslim world will plan this massive offensive against her. God calls Gog's plan "an evil plan." "Thus says the Lord God, 'It will come about on that day, that thoughts will come into your mind, and you will devise an evil plan'" (Ezek. 38:10).

This plan is especially heinous and evil because Gog plans this invasion as a surprise attack, knowing that Israel is at peace and highly susceptible to attack. Ezekiel 38:14 says, "Therefore, prophesy, son of man, and say to

Gog, 'Thus says the Lord GOD, "On that day when My people Israel are living securely, will you not know *it*?"'" Gog's knowledge of Israel's false security and tranquillity is the motivation for this invasion.

The purpose of the invasion is twofold. The first purpose is to totally destroy Israel. Ezekiel 38:9 says, "And you will go up, you will come like a storm; you will be like a cloud covering the land, you and all your troops, and many peoples with you." Verse 16 says, "And you will come up against My people Israel like a cloud to cover the land." Gog and his coalition will come to totally cover the land and annihilate the nation of Israel. They will advance across the land like a storm. The army will overrun all obstacles in its way as effortlessly as a cloud sailing across the sky. As we know, the total destruction of Israel has been the agenda of the Muslims ever since 1948.

The second purpose is to seize plunder and capture spoil. Israel's peaceful condition will produce great prosperity. Ezekiel 38:12 says that the people "have acquired cattle and goods, [and] live at the center of the world." The word *center* in this verse means "navel." Israel is considered by God to be the belly of the earth.

When Israel is under her covenant with the Antichrist, she will be able to eliminate military spending, something that is a tremendous drain on the Israeli economy. The elimination of military spending will cause an amazing increase in Israel's economic productivity and prosperity. This increase will be in addition to the already vast mineral wealth in the Dead Sea, some of the greatest mineral deposits in the world. Israel's Muslim neighbors will see these conditions coupled with Israel's lack of military defenses and will invade to totally destroy the Jews and plunder their nation.

Gog versus the United Nations

While Gog is devising this evil plan and beginning to attack, some of the nations of the world will raise a protest to the actions. Ezekiel 38:13 says, "Sheba, and Dedan, and the merchants of Tarshish, with all its villages, will say to you, 'Have you come to capture spoil? Have you assembled your company to seize plunder, to carry away silver and gold, to take away cattle and goods, to capture great spoil?'"

The nations of the world will take note of Gog's action and will issue a protest, but the protest is only in the form of lip service. The action here reminds one of the impotence of world organizations like the United Nations that often bark but rarely back it up with any bite.

The specific nations mentioned here who question Gog's actions are "Sheba, and Dedan, and the merchants of Tarshish, with all its villages." Sheba and Dedan are not difficult to identify. They are located in the modern country of Saudi Arabia.

Tarshish, on the other hand, is not so simple to identify. However, the weight of authority is that Tarshish is ancient Tartessus in the present-day nation of Spain. This view is supported by both Brown-Driver-Briggs[81] and Gesenius.[82]

Tarshish was a wealthy, flourishing colony of the Phoenicians that exported silver, iron, tin, and lead (Ezek. 27:12). But note that Ezekiel refers to "Tarshish, with all its villages (38:13)." The better translation is "Tarshish with all its young lions." Young lions are often used in the Scripture to refer to energetic rulers. Therefore, the young lions who verbally oppose Gog's invasion are strong military and political leaders who act with Tarshish.

Does all of this have any relevance to the situation we see in the world today? I think it fits the present world political situation precisely. Who is the one Middle East nation who consistently sides with the West against the radical Islamic elements in that region of the world? The obvious answer is Saudi Arabia—ancient Sheba and Dedan.

Where was Tarshish in Ezekiel's day? It was in the farthest west regions of the known world, in Spain. As we know, Spain is in modern Europe. Tarshish, or modern Spain, could be used by Ezekiel to represent all of the western nations whom Saudi Arabia will join with in denouncing this invasion. The Bible clearly reveals that the great western power in the end times will be centered in the reunited Roman Empire. It is highly probable that Ezekiel used the far western colony of Tarshish to represent the end-time empire of the Antichrist.

This is consistent with what we have already seen in Daniel 9:27 and Revelation 6:2-4. The Antichrist and his

Saudi Arabian allies will protest this invasion because the Antichrist will be joined to Israel by the seven-year covenant when Gog moves into Israel like a storm. However, Gog and his allies will completely ignore the protests of other nations and relentlessly storm into the land of Israel. All human efforts to change his mind will be futile because there are unseen powers behind the scenes drawing Gog into the land of Israel.

The Invisible War

We have seen that Gog will devise his evil plan to destroy Israel in the last days, but who or what is the ultimate force behind this invasion? Does Gog make his own plans and do his own bidding, or are there unseen forces at work behind the scenes?

The Bible tells us clearly that Satan is the god of this world religiously and the prince of this world politically. Three times in the book of John, Jesus says that Satan is the prince of this world. In Matthew 4, when Satan tempted Jesus and offered him the kingdoms of the world if he would bow down and worship him, Jesus didn't refute the legitimacy of Satan's offer. Jesus knew that Satan has been given control over this world in the present age. We read in 1 John 5:19 that "the whole world lies *in the power of* the evil one."

Satan's authority, however, is not just some general authority in the earth. The Bible says that Satan and his demonic princes are at work behind the scenes in politics, controlling leaders and nations. In Daniel 10:12-21, two satanic princes are identified as the "prince of the kingdom of Persia" and "the prince of Greece." These princes are demonic agents assigned to the sponsorship and control of the affairs of the Persian and Greek realms. We can deduce from this that Satan has a subdivided administrative authority with the entire globe organized under principalities corresponding to earthly governments. These satanic princes are Satan's henchmen who carry out his will in influencing world leaders and nations to do his bidding.

In Isaiah 14 and Ezekiel 28, we find the clearest descriptions of the character of Satan. He is unmasked as the unseen power behind human rulers. In Isaiah 14, Isaiah is addressing the king of Babylon, and in Ezekiel 28 the king of Tyre is being directly addressed.

The book of Revelation also sheds light on this fascinating subject. In Revelation 13, Satan is pictured as the motivating power behind the Antichrist. Revelation 13:2, 4 says: "And the dragon gave him his power and his throne and great authority. . . . And they worshiped the dragon, because he gave his authority to the beast; and they worshiped the beast, saying, 'Who is like the beast, and who is able to wage war with him?'"

In Revelation 16:13-14, 16, Satan and his henchmen are presented as the ones who gather the nations together for the great conflagration at Armageddon:

> And I saw *coming* out of the mouth of the dragon and out of the mouth of the beast and out of the

mouth of the false prophet, three unclean spirits like frogs; for they are spirits of demons, performing signs, which go out to the kings of the whole world, to gather them together for the war of the great day of God, the Almighty. . . . And they gathered them together to the place which in Hebrew is called Har-Magedon.

Revelation 20:3, 7-8 states that one of Satan's primary functions is to "deceive the nations." Therefore, while Gog and his allies will believe that their relentless attack of Israel is for their own purposes, the Bible declares that behind the scenes Satan will be the instigator of Gog's evil plan.

Man Proposes, God Disposes

Gog will clearly be the agent of this invasion, and Satan will be a strong force behind it, but who is ultimately in control? Are Gog and Satan in control? Is God just waiting on the sidelines to see how it will all come out? Ezekiel declares undeniably that the directing force behind this invasion is God himself. Gog is only the agent, and Satan is only a secondary motivating power. In Ezekiel 38:4 God says, "And I will turn you about, and put hooks into your jaws, and I will bring you out." Like a ring in the nose of a captive or a great hook in the jaws of a crocodile, God will pull Gog and his allies out for this invasion when he is ready for them. Gog will do God's bidding and will act according to God's timetable.

In Ezekiel 38:8 God says, "After many days you will be summoned." Verse 16 says, "It will come about in the last days that I shall bring you against My land, in order that the nations may know Me." Ezekiel 39:2 says, "And I shall turn you around, drive you on, take you up from the remotest parts of the north, and bring you against the mountains of Israel."

This same truth is revealed in Revelation 16:12, which says, "And the sixth *angel* poured out his bowl upon the great river, the Euphrates; and its water was dried up, that the way might be prepared for the kings from the east." Before the demon spirits in Revelation 16:13-14 gather all the armies together for the great slaughter at Armageddon, God is going before them to prepare the way for the advancing armies. God is in control and will make certain that no nation misses its appointment with destiny.

Who is in control of this invasion against Israel? God Almighty! He summons Gog, draws Gog out, turns him around, and drives him on. Of course, the evil plan to attack Israel will originate in the mind of Gog, and Gog will freely act to accomplish his own evil goals. But God will be the directing force of the entire invasion.

This is a lesson that all the world needs to understand: The sovereign God is in control of the world. He alone rules in the kingdom of men. The greatest monarch who ever lived had to learn this lesson the hard way.

King Nebuchadnezzar, who ruled the world for forty-three years and built the great city of Babylon, was walking on the roof of his palace one day. Daniel 4:30 records that as Nebuchadnezzar surveyed the magnificent city he had built, he became bloated and inflated with pride and uttered these words, "Is this not Babylon the great, which I myself have built as a royal residence by the might of my power and for the glory of my majesty?" The Bible records in Daniel 4:31-32 that while these words were still in Nebuchadnezzar's mouth, God spoke to him and said, "King Nebuchadnezzar, to you it is declared: sovereignty has been removed from you, and you will be driven away from mankind, and your dwelling place *will be* with the beasts of the field. You will be given grass to eat like cattle, and seven periods of time will pass over you, until you recognize that the Most High is ruler over the realm of mankind, and bestows it on whomever He wishes."

The purpose of the judgment on Nebuchadnezzar was to show Nebuchadnezzar and the whole world that God is sovereign and that he will not share his glory with another. Daniel 4:17 records the purpose of Nebuchadnezzar's judgment: "In order that the living may know That the Most High is ruler over the realm of mankind, And bestows it on whom He wishes, And sets over it the lowliest of men." God wants all the living to know that he is the one who rules in the kingdom of men. God's absolute and total control of the kingdoms of this world is stated powerfully in Isaiah 40:15-17, 23-25:

> Behold, the nations are like a drop from a bucket,
> And are regarded as a speck of dust on the scales;
> Behold, He lifts up the islands like fine dust. Even

Lebanon is not enough to burn, Nor its beasts enough for a burnt offering. All the nations are as nothing before Him, They are regarded by Him as less than nothing and meaningless. . . . He *it is* who reduces rulers to nothing, Who makes the judges of the earth meaningless. Scarcely have they been planted, Scarcely have they been sown, Scarcely has their stock taken root in the earth, But He merely blows on them, and they wither, And the storm carries them away like stubble. "To whom then will you liken Me That I should be *his* equal?" says the Holy One.

The problem is that people become inflated with pride and climb up on the pedestal and declare themselves to be god over their petty little empires. Victor Hugo tells an interesting story concerning Napoléon and the Battle of Waterloo:

On the morning of the battle, the little dictator stood gazing upon the field of battle as he described to his commanding officer his strategy for that day's campaign.

"We will put the infantry here, the cavalry there, the artillery here. At the end of the day England will be at the feet of France and Wellington will be prisoner of Napoléon."

After a pause the commanding officer said, "But we must not forget that man proposes but God disposes."

With arrogant pride the little dictator stretched his body to full height and replied, "I want you to understand, sir, that Napoléon proposes and Napoléon disposes."

From that moment Waterloo was lost, for God sent rain and hail so that the troops of Napoléon could not maneuver as he had planned, and on the night of battle it was Napoléon who was prisoner of Wellington, and France was at the feet of England.[83]

Gog, like Napoléon, will imagine that he is the master of his fate and the captain of his soul. Yet he will ultimately learn the lesson that God rules in the kingdom of men but only when it's too late!

Conclusion

Having considered the preconditions that lead up to this invasion and the unseen powers that are at work behind the scenes controlling Gog and his coalition, let's now turn our attention to the invasion itself and its incredible climax. Let's see what happens when Gog meets God!

NINE

When Gog Meets God

IN June 1967, the nation of Israel conducted one of the most decisive campaigns in the annals of war. Israel's main enemy was Egypt, but Syria and Jordan also attacked Israel's borders. The Israeli army struck its enemies on June 5, 1967, and shattered them within six days. Syria and Jordan were dealt crippling blows, and Egypt's army and air force were decimated in the now-famous Six-Day War.

The Bible says that a day is coming when the Islamic world will once again invade the nation of Israel but this time on an even larger scale and under the leadership of Russia. However, this war will be even more amazing than the Six-Day War. Ezekiel 38–39 describes what we might call the "one-day war" because, when Gog and his Muslim allies invade Israel in the last days, God will totally destroy them through supernatural judgment.

The Great Slaughter

Gog and his allies will invade Israel in the last days with a massive, well-prepared army. Israel will be living in her land unprotected and unsuspecting. This will look like the biggest mismatch in military history. When Gog mounts his offensive, it will look like the nation of Israel is finished. It will look like Satan has finally achieved his purpose of destroying the seed of Abraham.

However, God is in control of the entire situation. Gog and his allies are under God's authority and cannot go one step beyond his purposes. In fact, as we learned in the last chapter, God is the one drawing and summoning Gog to meet his final destiny in the land of Israel. God will orchestrate the whole situation until it appears to be utterly hopeless for Israel, then he will intervene so that he may demonstrate to the entire world that he is without equal.

When God brings Gog into the land of Israel, Gog and his forces will cover the land of Israel like a storm or a cloud covering the land (Ezek. 38:9, 16). In proud, inflated confidence, Gog and his allies will move in for the kill. They will look invincible. But God will intervene on behalf of his people:

> "And it will come about on that day, when Gog comes against the land of Israel," declares the Lord GOD, "that My fury will mount up in My anger. And in My zeal and in My blazing wrath"
> (Ezek. 38:18-19).

Notice the words God uses: "My fury," "My anger," "My zeal," and "My blazing wrath." God will pour out his vengeance on Gog like a flood.

God will use four primary means to destroy Gog and his army. The first is a great earthquake:

> I declare *that* on that day there will surely be a great earthquake in the land of Israel. And the fish of the sea, the birds of the heavens, the beasts of the field, all the creeping things that creep on the earth, and all the men who are on the face of the earth will shake at My presence; the mountains also will be thrown down, the steep pathways will collapse, and every wall will fall to the ground (Ezek. 38:19-20).

God will send an earthquake of unparalleled strength to the land of Israel to wipe out the invading horde.

The second means God will use to annihilate Gog will be infighting among the different troops:

> "And I shall call for a sword against him on all My mountains," declares the Lord GOD. "Every man's sword will be against his brother" (Ezek. 38:21).

Apparently, when the earthquake hits the land and the mountains are thrown down and the steep pathways collapse, Gog's army will break into chaos and confusion. His great invading force which looked invincible will turn against itself. Remember, Gog's army will be made up of troops from many nations: Russia, the Muslim nations of central Asia, Turkey, Iran, Egypt, the Sudan, and Libya. When God violently shakes the land and the troops fall into confusion, they will begin to kill one another. It is likely that in anger, frustration, and confusion, the armies of each of these nations will turn against one another. Troops in this army will speak Russian, Turkic, Arabic, and Farsi. When mass confusion breaks out, soldiers will probably begin killing anyone who does not speak their language. This will be the largest occurrence of death by "friendly fire" the world has ever seen.

The third means God will use to decimate Gog is pestilence or plagues: "And with pestilence and with blood I shall enter into judgment with him" (Ezek. 38:22).

The word used here for pestilence once described the divine plague on Pharaoh's livestock in Exodus 9:13. God will visit Gog and his troops with a horrible plague that will add to the misery and devastation already inflicted.

The final, climactic judgment God will use to eradicate Gog's horde will be fire and brimstone from heaven: "And I shall rain on him, and on his troops, and on the many peoples who are with him, a torrential rain, with hailstones, fire, and brimstone" (Ezek. 38:22).

Sodom and Gomorrah are two of the world's most well-known cities. These wicked cities became infamous when God poured out fire and brimstone on them and blotted them out because of their heinous sin. To this day people look for the ruins of these two cities, but God so completely wiped them out that the ruins have never been found. Just as God poured out fire and brimstone on Sodom and Gomorrah, he will devastate Gog and his allies, only on a vastly greater scale.

God will not only send fire upon the armies of Gog but will also pour out fire on Gog's homeland and headquarters in Magog. "And I shall send fire upon Magog and those who inhabit the coastlands in safety; and they will know that I am the LORD" (Ezek. 39:6).

Millions of people will be wiped off the face of the earth in a moment of time!

Here Lies Gog

The destruction of Gog is not the end of the story. Ezekiel goes on in 39:4-24 to set forth the results or aftermath of Gog's devastation. The aftermath primarily consists of two events: the burial of the dead bodies and the feeding of the birds and beasts on the carrion.

The extent of the slaughter can be seen from the fact that it will take seven months to bury all the bodies of the slain to cleanse the land:

> And it will come about on that day that I shall give Gog a burial ground there in Israel, the valley of those who pass by east of the sea, and it will block off the passers-by. So they will bury Gog there with all his multitude, and they will call *it* the valley of Hamon-Gog. For seven months the house of Israel will be burying them in order to cleanse the land (Ezek. 39:11-12).

The corpses will be buried east of the Dead Sea in ancient Moab, or the modern nation of Jordan. "Those who pass by east" is probably a proper name describing the mountains of Abarim east of the Dead Sea. Therefore, Gog's burial will be in "the valley of those who pass by east," or the Valley of Abarim across the Dead Sea.

The total number of corpses that will be gathered will be so great that the "valley of travelers" will be blocked. Due to the number of corpses, the name of the valley will be changed to Hamon-gog, which means "the valley of the hordes of Gog." The only piece of land Gog will claim in the land of Israel will be his burial plot! Gog will set out to bury Israel, but God will bury Gog!

Another detail is given to emphasize the vast proportions of the catastrophe. After the initial cleanup operation, squads of men will be employed to search the land for additional corpses.

> And they will set apart men who will constantly pass through the land, burying those who were passing through, even those left on the surface of the ground, in order to cleanse it. At the end of seven months they will make a search. And as those who pass through the land pass through and anyone sees a man's bone, then he will set up a marker by it until the buriers have buried it in the valley of Hamon-Gog. And even *the* name of *the* city will be

Hamonah. So they will cleanse the land (Ezek.
39:14-16).

As these cleanup squads go through the land, they will
set up markers wherever they see a human bone. When
the gravediggers come through the land, they will see the
markers and take the remains to the valley of Hamon-gog
for burial. The cleansing operation will be so extensive
that a town will be established in the valley at the grave-
sites to aid those who are cleansing the land. The name of
the town is Hamonah, which is a form of the word *hordes*.

The Great Supper

The second result of the destruction of Gog is even more
horrible and gruesome than the massive burial operation.
The carnage that results from the slaughter will provide a
great feast for the birds of the air and the beasts of the field.
God refers to the carnage as "My sacrifice" and "My table"
to which he invites the birds and the beasts as his guests:

"You shall fall on the mountains of Israel, you and
all your troops, and the peoples who are with you; I
shall give you as food to every kind of predatory
bird and beast of the field. You will fall on the open
field; for it is I who have spoken," declares the Lord
GOD. . . . "And as for you, son of man, thus says the
Lord GOD, 'Speak to every kind of bird and to every
beast of the field, "Assemble and come, gather from
every side to My sacrifice which I am going to sacrifice for you, as a great sacrifice on the mountains of

Israel, that you may eat flesh and drink blood. You shall eat the flesh of mighty men, and drink the blood of the princes of the earth, as *though they were* rams, lambs, goats, and bulls, all of them fatlings of Bashan. So you will eat fat until you are glutted, and drink blood until you are drunk, from My sacrifice which I have sacrificed for you. And you will be glutted at My table with horses and charioteers, with mighty men and all the men of war," declares the Lord God'" (Ezek. 39:4-5, 17-20).

A similar scene is pictured in Revelation 19:17-18 after the final battle of this age at Armageddon:

And I saw an angel standing in the sun; and he cried out with a loud voice, saying to all the birds which fly in midheaven, "Come, assemble for the great supper of God; in order that you may eat the flesh of kings and the flesh of commanders and the flesh of mighty men and the flesh of horses and of those who sit on them and the flesh of all men, both free men and slaves, and small and great."

This is the ultimate humiliation and degradation for proud human rulers. Both Gog with his army and then the Antichrist in Revelation 19 will be slaughtered by God and given as sacrifices to the animals and birds. Daniel 4:37 says of God, "He is able to humble those who walk in pride." He alone is God and he will not give his glory to another!

Conclusion

The result of Gog's invasion into Israel is obviously total devastation. However, God's fierce judgment in these chapters raises another important question: Why would God judge humanity with blazing anger? This is an important question to answer because it involves the character and nature of God. Is God really a God of love and mercy? Does God have a purpose behind his actions, or does he act in an arbitrary and capricious manner?

TEN

God's Glorious Purpose

H AVING considered who will be involved in this great invasion and what will happen before, during, and after the invasion, the next question we must consider is the *why* question. Answering the *why* question concerning any matter is often the most difficult. This is especially true when it comes to determining why God acts as he does in certain circumstances. Frequently, we never know why and are left to trust God that he is sovereign and always does what is right. However, in Ezekiel 38–39 God has been pleased to tell us why the devastation of Gog and his allies will occur.

The answer to the *why* question in these chapters is threefold: for God to bring glory to himself, for God to redeem sinful people, and for God to begin the final restoration of Israel. Of course, these three purposes are deeply interrelated, but we will consider them individually.

To God Be the Glory

The first reason for the destruction of Gog and his horde is to bring glory to God. God does not help Israel because she deserves his help but because his reputation is on the line. He acts to vindicate his own holy name and show forth his power. God clearly states his purpose in acting to deliver Israel in Ezekiel 36:22-24, 32:

> "Therefore, say to the house of Israel, 'Thus says the Lord GOD, "It is not for your sake, O house of Israel, that I am about to act, but for My holy name, which you have profaned among the nations where you went. And I will vindicate the holiness of My great name which has been profaned among the nations, which you have profaned in their midst. Then the nations will know that I am the LORD," declares the Lord GOD, "when I prove Myself holy among you in their sight. For I will take you from the nations, gather you from all the lands, and bring you into your own land. . . . I am not doing *this* for your sake," declares the Lord GOD, "let it be known to you. Be ashamed and confounded for your ways, O house of Israel!"'"

In Ezekiel 38:23 God says, "And I shall magnify Myself, sanctify Myself, and make Myself known in the sight of many nations; and they will know that I am the LORD." In Ezekiel 39:13 God says, "*On* the day that I glorify Myself." In Ezekiel 39:21 God says, "And I shall set My glory among the nations; and all the nations will see

My judgment which I have executed, and My hand which I have laid on them."

God will use this terrible slaughter to show forth his power and to show rebellious people that he alone is God and that beside him there is no other!

A Sign to the Nations

While the Bible is clear that God's greatest purpose in human history is to bring glory to himself, one way that God accomplishes that purpose is by redeeming sinful humans by his grace. In the destruction of Gog, these two purposes will be simultaneously achieved. God will bring glory to himself by vindicating his holy name, but he will also use this judgment as a great sign to convert multitudes of Gentiles during the Tribulation period.

This purpose is stated over and over again in Ezekiel 38–39: "that the nations may know Me" (38:16); "and make Myself known in the sight of many nations; and they will know that I am the LORD" (38:23); "and they will know that I am the LORD" (39:6); "And the nations will know that I am the Lord" (39:7); "And I shall set My glory among the nations; and all the nations will see My judgment which I have executed, and My hand which I have laid on them" (39:21).

Revelation declares that the multitude of saved Gentiles will be so great that they cannot be counted:

> After these things I looked, and behold, a great multitude, which no one could count, from every nation

and *all* tribes and peoples and tongues, standing before the throne and before the Lamb, clothed in white robes, and palm branches *were* in their hands. . . . And I said to him, "My lord, you know." And he said to me, "These are the ones who come out of the great tribulation, and they have washed their robes and made them white in the blood of the Lamb" (Rev. 7:9, 14).

One of the means God will use to convert this multitude will be the incontrovertible demonstration of his power against Gog. God in his mercy and grace will use the awe-inspiring judgment of Gog as a sign to convince many unbelievers that he alone is the true God.

The Beginning of the End

Another purpose that God will achieve through his judgment on Gog will be the beginning of the final restoration of Israel. This supernatural intervention by God will be a sign not only to the Gentiles but to the Jews as well. God will use this event to bring about the repentance of many of the Jewish people. Ezekiel 39:7, 22 says:

And My holy name I shall make known in the midst of My people Israel; and I shall not let My holy name be profaned anymore. . . . And the house of Israel will know that I am the LORD their God from that day onward.

With the destruction of Gog, God will begin to bring about Israel's final restoration. "I shall not let My Holy name be profaned anymore" doesn't mean from the exact moment of the destruction of Gog that God will never let his holy name be profaned. It would be impossible for God to say this during the Tribulation period. What this statement means is that from that point he will begin to act openly against those who profane his name without worry of consequences. After the destruction of Gog in the Tribulation period, God will no longer let people profane his holy name with impunity. From that point on, profaning God's name will bring dire consequences as we read in Revelation 6–19.

In Ezekiel 37 the vision of the valley of dry bones pictures the final regathering and restoration of the nation of Israel. Clearly, the first step in Israel's final restoration was her regathering in 1948, and the climax of that restoration will be the second coming of Christ when he comes to sit on David's throne to rule the earth. However, between 1948 and the Second Coming, God will use many events to bring about the conversion of his people. Some of the events are the sealing of the 144,000 Jews (Rev. 7), the ministry of the two witnesses (Rev. 11), and the persecution by the Antichrist (Rev. 12–13).

Another event God will use to bring about the final restoration of his people is the destruction of Gog and his mighty army. Ezekiel 39:25 says that the destruction of Gog signals the beginning of the final restoration of Israel: "Therefore thus says the Lord GOD, 'Now I shall restore the fortunes of Jacob, and have mercy on the whole house of Israel; and I shall be jealous for My holy name.'"

Like many times in the Old Testament, God will allow Israel's enemy to advance to the point where victory seems within his grasp, and then at the last moment, God will miraculously intervene to deliver his people. This event will be so amazing and so clearly supernatural that through it God will make his holy name known in the land of Israel. The conversion of many in Israel will clearly signal the beginning of the end of Israel's suffering. The time of Israel's domination and chastisement by Gentile nations that began with Nebuchadnezzar in 605 B.C. is nearing its end.

The only question that now remains is when will Gog's invasion of Israel occur. When will this "beginning of the end" take place?

ELEVEN

Timing Is Everything

NOW that we know who will participate in this invasion and what will take place, the only question that remains is when it will occur. It is not a question of whether these events will be fulfilled. Ezekiel clearly says that his message is a message from almighty God. Therefore, the prophecy of Ezekiel 38–39 will be fulfilled exactly as God has said. The only issue in question is when God will bring it to pass. As we see the nations in these chapters beginning to come together, the evidence is overwhelming that it is soon, but how soon?

The General Identification of the Time

While the specific time of the invasion is difficult to determine, the general identification can be ascertained with certainty. Conservative Bible scholars generally agree that this invasion has not been fulfilled in the past but wholly awaits a future fulfillment. Several factors support this conclusion.

First, the phrase "latter years" (Ezek. 38:8) and the identical phrase "last days" (38:16) are both used to describe the time of this invasion. These phrases are used a total of fifteen times in the Old Testament. They are always used to refer to either the Tribulation period (Deut. 4:30; 31:29) or the Millennium (Isa. 2:2; Mic. 4:1). While these phrases do not specifically identify the time of the invasion, they do clearly indicate that the general time period is future even from our day.

Second, the setting of these chapters is important. Ezekiel 33–39 is one of four main divisions in this book, and this section deals with Israel's future restoration. Chapter 37 deals with restoration of an unbelieving Israel to the land. Chapter 40 begins a new section describing the millennial temple and sacrifices. Therefore, the invasion of Gog and Magog is placed sometime between the beginning of Israel's restoration to the land and the beginning of the Millennium.

Third, in chapters 38 and 39, Israel is pictured as gathered from the nations, inhabiting her own land, and dwelling securely. While these factors are subject to different interpretations, they seem to indicate that the events in these chapters transpire after the beginning of the restoration of the nation of Israel in chapter 37. Moreover, they could indicate that the invasion occurs after the formulation of the seven-year covenant made between Israel and the Antichrist as described in Daniel 9:27.

It is therefore concluded that the attack by Gog and Magog must take place in the future when God is bringing about the final restoration of Israel.

The Specific Identification of the Time

Within the general time period established above, there are six main views concerning the time of the invasion:

1. before the Tribulation period (before the Rapture);
2. near the beginning of the Tribulation;
3. near the middle of the Tribulation;
4. at the end of the Tribulation;
5. at the beginning of the Millennium; or
6. at the end of the Millennium.

The timing of the invasion described by Ezekiel has been related to nearly every major prophetic event. Consequently, the specific events in these chapters must now be examined more carefully in order to determine the specific time of this attack. In examining these events, each of the six views will be presented, and the primary arguments for and against each will be considered.

Before the Tribulation (Before the Rapture)

Those who hold this view believe that the words "living securely," which are used in this chapter three times (Ezek. 38:8, 11, 14), are explainable only if the Tribulation period has not yet begun.

While this view is possible, it must be rejected for

three reasons. First, this view nullifies the New Testament teaching of the imminence of the Rapture. The writers of the New Testament consistently implore their readers to be looking for the coming of Christ to translate them to heaven (1 Thess. 1:10; Titus 2:13). Believers in the church age are told to look for the coming of Christ, not signs. If the events in Ezekiel 38–39 must occur before the Rapture, then the Rapture of the church cannot happen at any moment but must wait for the fulfillment of this event.

Second, the time of this prophecy is clearly in the "latter years" or "last days," which we have already seen in the Old Testament always refers to the Tribulation or the Millennium.

Third, this prophecy is in the restoration section of the book of Ezekiel and, therefore, cannot be fulfilled before Israel even enters into the seven-year covenant with the Antichrist, or "the prince who is to come," which is predicted in Daniel 9:26-27.

Near the Beginning of the Tribulation

Another view that is held by many scholars is that this invasion will occur near the beginning of the Tribulation period when Israel is living "securely" under the covenant with the Antichrist or "the prince who is to come" (Ezek. 38:8, 11; Dan. 9:26-27).[84] Gog and his confederates will see the prosperity that abounds in Israel under this covenant and will come against her seeking spoil, only to be destroyed by God on the mountains of Israel.

Some view this destruction as a sign to the nations and the key to the conversion of the 144,000 Jews early in the Tribulation. This view explains the use of the weapons as fuel for seven years (Ezek. 39:9-10) because the seven-year period fits exactly with the remaining seven years of the Tribulation period. This view also explains the seven-month cleansing period for the land of Israel mentioned in Ezekiel 39:12, which follows the destruction since the period of cleansing would be complete before the Antichrist breaks the covenant with Israel.

While this view has much to commend it, it is rejected because it places this invasion too early in the Tribulation period. If the invaders of Ezekiel 38–39 are equivalent to the king of the south and the king of the north from Daniel 11:11-12 (see chapters 6 and 7), then this invasion is not at the beginning of the Tribulation but near the middle.

The End of the Tribulation

Many excellent Bible students have viewed this invasion as part of the final conflagration of nations against Jerusalem described in Zechariah 12–14.[85] In Zechariah 14:1-4 we are told of the gathering of all nations against Jerusalem, an event that takes place just prior to the manifestation of Jesus Christ as King when his feet shall stand upon the Mount of Olives. The invading horde in Ezekiel 38–39 is included in the great invading force associated with Armageddon; therefore, the onslaught depicted in this chapter will take place toward the close of the great Tribulation.

Another strong point that supports this view is the bird supper that is recorded in Ezekiel 39:4, 17-20 and a similar event in Revelation 19:17-18 during the aftermath of Armageddon when the King of kings returns.

There are three arguments against this view that render it improbable, if not impossible. First, the text clearly states that this invasion will occur when Israel is "living securely" (38:8, 11, 14), "at rest" (38:11), and in "unwalled villages . . . living without walls, and having no bars or gates" (38:11). This description does not harmonize with the rest of Scripture, where the last half of the Tribulation period, or seventieth week, is characterized by satanic attack upon the nation of Israel (Rev. 12:14-17).

Another objection to this view is that the passage in Ezekiel does not mention a military battle other than the fact that the invaders kill one another. The destruction is primarily by divine intervention through a convulsion of nature (Ezek. 38:20-23). In the conflagration of Armageddon, there is a great battle fought between the Lord with his hosts and the assembled nations in which the King of kings slays his enemies with the word of his mouth and emerges as the victor (Rev. 19:11-15).

Additionally, in Ezekiel 38–39 the invasion is limited to Gog or the king of the north and his allies, which are limited in number. In Zechariah 14 and Revelation 19, all the nations of the earth are gathered together for the great slaughter.

At the Beginning of the Millennium

This view, which is not widely held today, is that the invasion in Ezekiel 38–39 will occur during the Messianic age, or transition period between the end of the Tribulation period and the actual establishment or inauguration of the millennial kingdom.[86] Those who hold to this view maintain that the invasion will occur after the destruction of the reunited Roman Empire in its final ten-kingdom form and the judgment of its leader, the Antichrist, and his lieutenant, the false prophet. The other nations who were not part of the final conflagration at Armageddon will then gather for an assault. This assault will be led by Gog and the northern confederacy.

Support for this view is drawn from two main areas: the context of these chapters and the conditions in Israel that are set forth in chapter 38.

Those who hold this view observe that these chapters are in the restoration section of 33 through 39. They further note that in the preceding chapters, especially chapter 37, Israel is viewed as fully restored to her land with all the covenants fulfilled.

The second argument in favor of this view is that in Ezekiel 38 there are several statements that seem to refer to millennial conditions: "land that is restored from the sword" (38:8), "*whose inhabitants* have been gathered from many nations" (38:8), "living securely" (38:8, 11,

14), and "the people who are gathered from the nations, who have acquired cattle and goods" (38:12). The exact phrase "live securely" is often used in Scripture in prophetic passages to refer to the peaceful conditions that will prevail during the Millennium (Ezek. 28:26; 34:25, 28).

This view, like the other views that have been considered, has several strengths; however, it too must be rejected. Three main objections will be presented. First, while it is true that these chapters are in the restoration section, the perspective of Ezekiel 33 through 39 is not in any sense a chronological progression but rather thematic. Different aspects of Israel's restoration are presented in each chapter. Therefore, it is not necessary that one view chapters 38–39 as following the restoration in chapters 36 and 37 but rather as presenting a different aspect of Israel's restoration.

Second, the consistent witness of Scripture is that the wicked will be destroyed when Christ returns to the earth. Jeremiah 25:32-33 states that the Lord will destroy all the wicked of the earth at his return:

> Thus says the LORD of hosts, "Behold, evil is going forth From nation to nation, And a great storm is being stirred up From the remotest parts of the earth. And those slain by the LORD on that day shall be from one end of the earth to the other. They shall not be lamented, gathered, or buried; they shall be like dung on the face of the ground."

Revelation 19:15-18 amplifies this picture. It seems impossible to think of such a horde as described in Ezekiel escaping the destruction at Christ's coming to rise up against Israel again in such a short time.

Third, the strongest objection against this view is that the maximum time period that can be scripturally supported between Christ's return and the actual establishment of his kingdom is seventy-five days according to Daniel 12:11-12. According to many, this time period is only forty-five days. It seems inconceivable that Israel could be fully restored to the land with all the covenants fulfilled, that Israel could be wealthy and living in millennial peace, and that this vast horde of invading nations could assemble their massive army and invade Israel all in a period of forty-five to seventy-five days. These events would certainly take a lengthy period of time.

At the End of the Millennium

Perhaps the simplest solution to the problem is to equate this invasion with the postmillennial invasion in Revelation 20:7-9. Ezekiel 38–39 and Revelation 20:8 are the only two places in the Bible where Gog and Magog are mentioned in Scripture. Since these are the only two mentions of these names and both passages describe an invasion of Israel by a vast horde of nations, it seems logical to equate these two invasions with one another.

Many of the same arguments used to support this view are used to support the view that this invasion occurs at the beginning of the Millennium: the context of the chapters and the conditions in Israel ("living securely," "the land that is restored from the sword," etc.).

Traditionally, this view has been refuted by pointing out the discrepancies between the accounts in Ezekiel and Revelation. Some of these variants are that the invading armies are different; that Ezekiel mentions the mountains of Israel, whereas John refers to the city of Jerusalem; that John mentions Satan, but Satan is not mentioned in Ezekiel; and that in Ezekiel the bodies are buried, but in Revelation they are consumed entirely. However, those who hold to this view argue that in both accounts the armies come from all four directions, and they discount the other discrepancies by pointing out that John leaves out many details because he is only summarizing Ezekiel's lengthy, more detailed account.

While it is true that many of the usual objections that are raised against this view are inconclusive, there are three arguments against this view that render it impossible. First, as previously noted, these chapters are set in the context of restoration (Ezek. 33–39) followed by a description of the millennial temple and sacrifices (Ezek. 40–48). The invasion in chapters 38 and 39 is a part of Israel's restoration that will occur chronologically before the millennial kingdom is officially established. In Revelation 20, the events fit chronologically after the Millennium.

Second, the disposal of the bodies and the weapons is against this view. Ezekiel 39 states that it requires seven months to bury the bodies of the slain (39:12, 14) and seven years to burn the weapons of the armies (39:9). In Revelation 20, the next event after the battle of Gog and Magog is the Great White Throne Judgment (20:11-15). In this judgment all of the unsaved will stand before God in resurrected bodies to face their sentence. It seems illogical for Israel to spend seven months burying the dead only to have them immediately raised out of the graves and brought before the bar of God.

The next event in Revelation after the Great White Throne Judgment is the eternal state (Rev. 21–22). It also seems illogical for Israel to be burning wood for fuel during the eternal state. Those who hold the postmillennial view would answer these objections by saying that there is a long transition period between the battle of Gog and Magog and the great white throne and eternal state. However, why would God, who has once and for all showed humanity's utter depravity during the Millennium, allow a lengthy transition period in which more people would reject him? The battle of Gog and Magog seems to be the final climactic battle between God and Satan that consummates human history. Having once and for all proved his absolute right to rule, God begins to judge all unbelievers. There is no need for a lengthy transition between the battle of Gog and Magog and the great white throne.

Third, Ezekiel 39:7 reveals God's purpose in destroying the invaders: "And My holy name I shall make known in the midst of My people Israel; and I shall not let My holy name be profaned anymore. And the nations will know that I am the Lord, the Holy One in Israel." This stated purpose makes it clear that this divine judgment is part of Israel's restoration during the Tribulation, not after the Millennium. Why would God need to prove to Israel that he is the sovereign ruler if they had been enjoying the personal presence of the Messiah for over one thousand years?

This discussion immediately raises an important question: If this is not the invasion of Ezekiel 38–39, then how is John using the phrase Gog and Magog in Revelation? One interpretation is that John gives this phrase a stereotyped usage just as we today use Waterloo to describe a disastrous defeat. While this explanation is helpful, the best interpretation is that John's purpose in using the phrase Gog and Magog to describe the postmillennial invasion is to graphically emphasize the similarities between the two events. Four similarities are emphasized:

1. Both involve a confederation of nations that come from the "four corners of the earth";
2. both occur when Israel is "living securely" in the land;
3. both have the same object—to destroy Israel; and
4. both are destroyed by supernatural judgment.

Therefore, notwithstanding the mention of Gog and Magog in both of these passages and the similarities between the two events, the two invasions are distinct from one another and separated by one thousand years.

Near the Middle of the Tribulation

You are probably wondering by now, if none of these views are correct, when in the world will this invasion take place? As you can probably guess, the preferred view has been saved until the last. The view that best explains all of the details of these chapters is that the invasion occurs near the middle of the Tribulation period. This view, like the others, is not without problems, but it seems to be the best interpretation when correlated with the rest of Scripture.

The peace and security Israel experiences in Ezekiel 38:8, 11, 14 is best explained as occurring in the first half of the Tribulation period when the seven-year treaty with the Antichrist is in force. This peace is broken, however, when Gog and Magog invade the land seeking spoil. Gog and his allies are viewed as the king of the north and the king of the south in Daniel 11:40. When Gog and his allies launch their attack against the Antichrist and his ally Israel, the Antichrist responds with a counterattack that eventuates in his invasion into Israel and the severance of his covenant with Israel. Therefore, it is the invasion of Gog that eliminates the Russian-Muslim threat and prepares the way for the Antichrist's worldwide rule, precipitates the breaking of the treaty with Israel, and initiates the second half of the Tribulation period. Therefore, as you can see, this event is one of the key events in the Tribulation period. For this reason, Ezekiel 38–39 is a vitally important section to understand!

There are four central arguments in support of this

view. First, Israel is pictured in these chapters three times as "living securely" (Ezek. 38:8, 11, 14). While this phrase is used by proponents of other views, it will also be true of Israel during the first half of the Tribulation period when the nation is living under her seven-year covenant with the Antichrist (Dan. 9:27).

Second, the purpose of God's destruction of the invaders is to provide a sign to both the nations and Israel (Ezek. 39:6-7, 13, 21-23). This purpose is in harmony with the other Tribulation judgments that are meted out by God to show the Gentiles and Jews that he is sovereign.

Third, this passage correlates with the invasion of the king of the south and the king of the north in Daniel 11:40. This verse says, "And at the end time the king of the South will collide with him, and the king of the North will storm against him with chariots, with horsemen, and with many ships; and he will enter countries, overflow *them,* and pass through." While many have held that Gog and Magog are synonymous with only the king of the north, it seems best to include both the king of the south and the king of the north in this invasion. Ezekiel includes the Sudan and Libya in this invasion, which are nations to the south of Israel (the king of the south). These two nations are also mentioned by Daniel along with Egypt as nations the Antichrist attacks in his mop-up operation (Dan. 11:42-43). The difference is that Ezekiel refers to each of the invaders individually, whereas Daniel refers to the invaders as belonging to two main companies—the king of the south and the king of the north. It is interesting that Ezekiel and Daniel were contemporaries and both describe this invasion in roughly the same terms. Isaiah and Micah were contemporaries, and they both speak of this eschatological invader as "the Assyrian" (Isa. 31:8-9; Mic. 5:5).

This invasion by Gog is the trigger that breaks the delicate peace that existed in the first half of the Tribulation and sets off the great Tribulation. Since Daniel 9:27 clearly declares that the Antichrist breaks his seven-year covenant with Israel at the midpoint and the invasion of the king of the south and the king of the north are the cause of the breaking of the covenant (Dan. 11:30-41), we may conclude that the invasion in Ezekiel 38–39 occurs just before the middle of the Tribulation period.

Therefore, since this invasion precipitates the breaking of the covenant and the Antichrist's rise to worldwide authority, it is also the breaking of the second seal in Revelation 6:3-4 when peace is taken from the earth. The seals that follow—famine, death, and the martyrization of believers—all begin at the middle of the Tribulation as well.

Fourth, Ezekiel 38:17 says, "Are you the one of whom I spoke in former days through My servants the prophets of Israel, who prophesied in those days for *many* years that I would bring you against them?" This statement indicates that former prophets of Israel had also spoken of this eschatological vision. While there is no other direct reference to Gog and Magog in the Old Testament, it seems that the invasion was referred to by Isaiah as "the Assyrian" (Isa. 31:8-9), by Joel as "the northern army" (Joel 2:20), by Micah as "the Assyrian" (Mic. 5:5), and by Daniel as "the king of the South and the king of the North" (Dan. 11:40) (if Daniel can be referred to as a former prophet). Those who hold to other views concerning the chronology of this invasion have a difficult time finding former prophecies to sustain their view.

Fifth, the invasion in Ezekiel 38–39 may be linked with the casting of Satan from heaven in Revelation 12 near the middle of the Tribulation period. The invasion may be the first act Satan instigates in persecuting Israel. By moving Gog and his allies against Israel, Satan sets in motion all the events that lead to the Antichrist's invasion and persecution of Israel, and the ultimate demise of all Gentile powers at the return of Jesus Christ.

As previously noted, this view also has some problems. Three of the main objections will be considered.

One common objection is that, if this invasion and destruction occurs near the middle of the Tribulation, how will the Jews be able to spend seven months burying the dead while they are being persecuted by the Beast in the land? While this objection does have some merit, it is not fatal to this view. Daniel 11:41-43 states that after the Antichrist invades Israel he immediately initiates a southern campaign against Egypt, Libya, and the Sudan to consolidate his authority. It could be that it is during his brief absence that the Jews will bury the dead. Moreover, whether there is persecution or not, these dead bodies will need to be disposed of in some manner, and it is not inconceivable that the Jews will organize to accomplish the task.

Second, it is frequently objected that the king of the south and the king of the north attack the Antichrist, not Israel (Dan. 11:40). Ezekiel specifically states that Gog and Magog attack Israel (38:11-12). One way to solve this problem is to view the offensive as an attack upon the Antichrist and Israel since the two are joined by covenant. Another possible solution is that Ezekiel and Daniel are not contradicting one another but complementing one another. Ezekiel emphasizes the attack against Israel in his restoration prophecy and gives much more detail. Daniel 7–12, on the other hand, focuses on the Antichrist and his person and work, and states that Gog and his allies attack him.

Third, Ezekiel 39:9 states that Israel will burn the weapons of the invaders for seven years. Many have contended that, if this took place in the middle of the Tribulation, the Jews, who would then be under persecution, would need the weapons for defense rather than firewood. However, it is also true that these Jews who will flee into the wilderness will need firewood for fuel during the Tribulation, and it is likely that the abundance of despoiled weapons will provide a ready source for them.

Conclusion

Having shown the strengths and weaknesses of all of the views, the most tenable view is that Gog and all his allies will invade Israel near the middle of the Tribulation period. While none of the views is without problems, this seems to be the view that has the fewest problems, that best fits the overall context, and that harmonizes most clearly with the rest of Scripture.

Now that the timing of this invasion has been established, it is time to look at our world today, especially the former Soviet republics, Russia, Turkey, Iran, Libya, the Sudan, and Egypt, to see how these nations are aligning themselves for the coming invasion of Israel. This invasion will not take place until the middle of the Tribulation period, but the shadows of this invasion are already being cast across the Middle East!

TWELVE

Setting the Stage

Look among the nations! Observe! Be astonished!
Wonder! Because I am doing something in your
days—You would not believe if you were told.
(Hab. 1:5)

The history of mankind is filled with war and destruction. From the time of Nimrod in Genesis 10 and the first war recorded in the Bible in Genesis 14, human history has been strewn with the wreckage of war.

According to the *Canadian Army Journal,* a conscientious study of history has revealed the following figures concerning man's evil, warlike nature:

Since 3600 B.C. the world has known only 292 years of peace. During this period there have been 14,531 wars, large and small, in which 3,640,000,000 people have been killed. The value of the destruction would pay for a golden belt around the world about 100 miles wide and 33 feet thick! Since 650 B.C. there have been 1,656 arms races, only 16 of which have not ended in war! The remainder have terminated in the economic collapse of the countries concerned.

Since the world cast out the "Prince of Peace," the Lord Jesus Christ, by crucifying Him 2,000 years ago, there has not been one year without a war. In fact, in the last 500 years England has engaged in 78 wars; France, 71 wars; the Netherlands, 23; Spain, 64; Australia, 52; Germany, 23; Italy, 25; China, 11; Denmark, 20; Sweden, 26; Poland, 30; Russia, 61; Turkey, 43; and Japan, 9. European nations alone engaged in 74 wars during the lifetime of the first generation born in the twentieth century. Even America with its short history has engaged in 13 wars. And so, "man's inhumanity to man" continues![87]

On the basis of the computation in the *Moscow Gazette*, Gustave Valbert in his day could report that "from the year 1496 B.C. to A.D. 1861 in 3,358 years there were 227 years of peace and 3,130 years of war, or 13 years of war to every year of peace. Within the last 3 centuries, there have been 286 wars in Europe." He added that from the year 1500 B.C. to A.D. 1860 more than eight thousand treaties of peace, meant to remain in force forever, were concluded. The average time they remained in force was two years.[88]

In August 1989 there were nineteen wars going on in the world, each taking the lives of more than one thousand people a year. We are all aware of the many armed conflicts currently going on in our world today. We see them every day on the news and in the newspaper. Our world truly is filled with wars and rumors of wars. However, the Bible tells us that the worst is yet to come! Jesus said that one of the signs of the end of the age, or the Tribulation period, will be wars and strife between nations: "And you will be hearing of wars and rumors of wars; see that you are not frightened, for *those things* must take place, but *that* is not yet the end. For nation will rise against nation, and kingdom against kingdom" (Matt. 24:6-7).

During the Tribulation period, human history will culminate in the great conflagration at Armageddon. The battle that sets the stage for the events of Armageddon and triggers the beginning of the great Tribulation is the invasion of Israel by Gog and his allies. But before we look at Gog's invasion and the coming campaign of Armageddon, we need to see the great alignment of nations that the Bible predicts in the last days.

The Alignment of Nations

Human warfare is nothing new for mankind. It is one of the chief characteristics of our sinful race. Therefore, the fact that there are many wars in our world today is not in itself an indication that we are nearing the time of the coming of Christ. However, the Bible, while it does predict a general state of warfare in the Tribulation period, also outlines specifically the political, geographical, and military divisions into which the world will be divided.

According to Bible prophecy, at least four great world powers will exist contemporaneously in the end times. The world will be divided into four great spheres of power.

The King of the North

The first of these powers is called the king of the north in the Bible. Daniel 11:40 says, "And the king of the North will storm against him with chariots, with horsemen, and with many ships." The king of the north is a military power that hails from the area north of the land of Israel. This power is the northern invader described in Ezekiel 38–39. As we have already seen, the northern nations who will invade Israel are Russia, the former central Asian republics of the Soviet Union, Turkey, and Iran. This great power bloc is being formed before our eyes. Iran and Turkey are the two major players who are wooing the newly formed Muslim nations in central Asia.

The King of the South

The second major power mentioned in Bible prophecy is the king of the south. Daniel 11:40 says, "And at the end time the king of the South will collide with him." Daniel 11:42-43 goes on to mention several nations that are located to the south of the nation of Israel: Egypt, the Sudan, and Libya. Two of these nations, the Sudan and Libya, are also referred to in Ezekiel 38:5. The king of the south, therefore, is a North African alliance of Muslim nations. Other African nations may be included in this bloc of nations, but there is no way to be certain on this point. At a minimum, this coalition is North African Muslim nations.

The King of the West

A third great power in the end times is the reunited Roman Empire, or what we might call the western confederacy or king of the west. The Bible never calls this power the king of the west, but this coalition is clearly the reunited Roman Empire, which will be centered in Europe, west of Israel.

Nebuchadnezzar's dream of the great image in Daniel 2 and Daniel's vision of the four beasts in Daniel 7 reveal that the historical Roman Empire, which fell apart in A.D. 476 in the west and A.D. 1453 in the east, will be reunited in the end times in a ten-kingdom form. These ten kingdoms will be ruled over by one tyrannical dictator described in Daniel 7:8 as the little horn, in Daniel 8:23 as "A king . . . Insolent and skilled in intrigue," in Daniel 9:26 as "the prince who is to come," and in Daniel 11:36-39 as the willful king.

The formation of the European Economic Community and the economic union of Europe that we see happening before our eyes are only the prelude to the political union of Europe under one powerful leader. David Lawday writing in *U.S. News and World Report* says:

> Ignore this, America, at your peril. The nations of Western Europe, whose quarrels have plunged the

world into war twice in this century, have swept
aside seemingly insurmountable obstacles to unity,
and with bottom-line disputes over money and deci-
sion making now behind them, they are fast locking
themselves together more tightly than Charlemagne,
Napoléon, or even Hitler ever contrived to do. . . .
There are arguments about what should follow, but
logically all this points toward a single currency that
would rival or outgun the dollar, and to a European
central bank similar to the U.S. Federal Reserve. . . .
The ultimate result would be some kind of common
European government, perhaps based on West Germany's low-profile federal system, which ensures the
autonomy of its separate states. As a Dutch government official observes, "Economic integration without political integration goes bankrupt in the end."
. . . Meanwhile, Europewide citizen support for an
overall European government is edging upward—to
53 percent, according to the latest polls—and the
authority vacuum may compel EEC leaders to fill it
faster than some now wish.[89]

The king of the west is coming!

The Kings of the East
The final sphere of power during the end times is called
in Revelation 16:12 the kings of the east: "And the sixth
angel poured out his bowl upon the great river, the
Euphrates; and its water was dried up, that the way
might be prepared for the kings from the east." The Bible
gives us no other information about this great power, but

we know from the information in this verse that the kings who make up this power come from east of the Euphrates River. This could include nations such as India, Afghanistan, Pakistan, and all the nations of the Orient, or Far East.

The Bible is clear that world power in the end times will be aligned into these four great divisions. Each of these four great powers will be drawn into the final series of conflicts known as the campaign of the great day of God, the Almighty. This military campaign is also known as the campaign of Armageddon.

The Campaign of Armageddon

The Bible declares that World War III is coming! The name the Bible gives for this war is the war of the great day of God, the Almighty (Rev. 16:14). The common designation among most people for this great time of bloodshed is the Battle of Armageddon.

The word translated as "war" in Revelation 16:14 is the Greek word *polemos,* which can refer either to a single military engagement or a battle or a war. The more common meaning is a war, state of war, or the process of war. In later use the word *mache* was used for an individual battle, whereas *polemos* designated a state of war.[90]

The events of Armageddon are described in the Bible not as one isolated battle fought near Mount Megiddo in the Valley of Megiddo but as a state of war that extends over a period of time. Therefore, the more accurate description would be the War or Campaign of Armageddon, instead of

149

the Battle of Armageddon. Clearly, the events of this campaign will culminate at the plain of Megiddo in northern Israel. But the military movements leading up to this final climax will extend over the last three and a half years of the Tribulation. The Campaign of Armageddon chronicles the attempts of the four great powers of the end times to gain ascendancy over the world.

The battleground for all of the military clashes mentioned in Bible prophecy is in or right around the nation of Israel. Israel will be repeatedly subjected to invading armies and will endure countless atrocities.

There will be five main invasions of the land of Israel during the Campaign of Armageddon. These invasions will sweep over the land of Israel in successive waves, leaving destruction and havoc in their wake.

Let's look at the main events of this campaign and each of the individual invaders in chronological order.

Invader #1

The first power to invade Israel in the last days will be the king of the south. This invasion is described in Daniel 11:40 and Ezekiel 38–39. As we have already seen, the king of the south is a North African coalition of nations, including Egypt, the Sudan, and Libya, who will invade Israel sometime just before the middle of the Tribulation period.

Invader #2

The second invader of Israel in the Tribulation period is the king of the north. According to Daniel 11:40 and Eze-

kiel 38–39, the king of the north invades Israel simultaneously with the king of the south. "And at the end time
the king of the South will collide with him, and the king
of the North will storm against him with chariots, with
horsemen, and with many ships" (Dan. 11:40). The king
of the south, the North African Muslim nations, will
invade Israel from the south while his northern allies,
Russia, the central Asian Muslim nations, Turkey, and
Iran, push into the land from the north.

As Ezekiel records, this massive horde of nations from
the north and south of Israel will be wiped off the face of
the earth by the blazing fury of Almighty God.

Invader #3
With the Middle Eastern and Russian threat removed, a
great power vacuum will result. Daniel 11:40 reveals that
the next invader into Israel is the king of the west, or the
Antichrist and his western confederacy. Daniel 11:40-41
says, "He will enter countries, overflow *them,* and pass
through. He will also enter the Beautiful Land, and many
countries will fall; but these will be rescued out of his hand:
Edom, Moab and the foremost of the sons of Ammon."

After entering the Beautiful Land, which is a clear reference to Israel, the Antichrist will take his army to the
south to mop up what is left of the forces of the king of
the south and to begin the consolidation of his empire.
"Then he will stretch out his hand against *other* countries, and the land of Egypt will not escape. But he will
gain control over the hidden treasures of gold and silver,

and over all the precious things of Egypt; and Libyans
and Ethiopians *will follow* at his heels" (Dan. 11:42-43).

While the Antichrist is down in North Africa consolidating his kingdom and plundering riches, he will hear
disturbing news from the north and east (Dan. 11:44).
The land directly to the north and east of North Africa is
Israel. Evidently, the Jews, realizing that they are probably his next prey, will stage an uprising against the Antichrist's power. This uprising will anger the Antichrist,
and he will leave North Africa to take care of the revolt in
Israel. When he enters the land of Israel, Daniel 11:44
says that he will devastate the land: "But rumors from the
East and from the North will disturb him, and he will go
forth with great wrath to destroy and annihilate many."

After taking control of Israel, the Antichrist will then establish his headquarters in the land of Israel. "And he will
pitch the tents of his royal pavilion between the seas and
the beautiful Holy Mountain" (Dan. 11:45). The seas mentioned here are the Dead Sea and the Mediterranean Sea. He
will set up his headquarters between these seas at "the beautiful Holy Mountain," or the city of Jerusalem. From Jerusalem the Antichrist will begin his three-and-a-half-year reign
of terror that is graphically described in the book of Daniel,
in 2 Thessalonians 2, and in Revelation 13.

Invader #4
Somewhere near the end of the three-and-a-half-year
reign of the Antichrist, he will begin to hear strong rum-
blings in the eastern part of his empire. After God has

poured out his wrath on the earth in successive waves of judgment from the seven seals and seven trumpets, the earth and its inhabitants will be left reeling. At that time the kings from the east will decide that they have had enough of the Antichrist's reign and that it is time for a change at the top.

Revelation 16:12-16 states that God will dry up the Euphrates River to provide easy access for this vast military horde from the east to enter the land of Israel and meet its fate at Har-Magedon.

As this huge Asiatic army draws near to the land of Israel, the Antichrist and his masses will gather to meet the challenge. However, sometime before the kings from the east and the Antichrist's forces engage one another, their attention will be drawn away from one another to another invader—the final invader!

Invader #5
Revelation 19 records the consummation of the campaign. Revelation 19:11-21 reveals that the final invader in the Campaign of Armageddon is none other than the King of kings and Lord of lords and his army from heaven. While the armies of the kings from the east and the Antichrist are preparing to do battle with one another, something will catch their eye that will turn their attention from one another and immediately cement them together as staunch allies. What event could possibly bring archenemies together so quickly? A common opponent!

As these enemies prepare to kill one another, a sign will appear in the heavens portending the second coming of Christ. Matthew 24:29-30 says, "But immediately after the tribulation of those days THE SUN WILL BE DARKENED, AND THE MOON WILL NOT GIVE ITS LIGHT, AND THE STARS WILL FALL from the sky, and the powers of the heavens will be shaken, and then the sign of the Son of Man will appear in the sky, and then all the tribes of the earth will mourn, and they will see the SON OF MAN COMING ON THE CLOUDS OF THE SKY with power and great glory."

The exact nature of this sign is not revealed in Matthew 24, but the best interpretation is that it is the shekinah glory, or brilliant shining, of the appearance of the King of kings. When these vast armies see this sign, they will instantly forget their animosity toward one another and turn it against God.

Revelation 19:19 says, "And I saw the beast and the kings of the earth and their armies, assembled to make war against Him who sat upon the horse, and against His army."

When Christ returns from heaven, it will be as if these nations shake their fist in God's face and repeat the words of Psalm 2:2-3, "The kings of the earth take their stand, And the rulers take counsel together Against the LORD and against His Anointed: 'Let us tear their fetters apart, And cast away their cords from us!'"

The consummation of the Campaign of Armageddon is powerfully sudden and quick. The Lord of glory will destroy this vast military force with nothing more than a spoken word: "And the beast was seized, and with him the false prophet who performed the signs in his presence, by which he deceived those who had received the mark of the beast and those who worshiped his image; these two were thrown alive into the lake of fire which burns with brimstone. And the rest were killed with the sword which came from the mouth of Him who sat upon the horse, and all the birds were filled with their flesh" (Rev. 19:20-21).

The same destiny for the Antichrist is revealed in 2 Thessalonians 2:8: "And then that lawless one will be revealed whom the Lord will slay with the breath of His mouth and bring to an end by the appearance of His coming."

Psalm 2:9 shows God's response to the foolish rebellion of the rulers gathered at Armageddon: "Thou shalt break them with a rod of iron, Thou shalt shatter them like earthenware." Christ's destruction of the armies gathered against his authority will be as effortless and complete as someone dashing a vessel of pottery into pieces with a royal scepter or battle mace.

With his coming the Lord Jesus will definitely establish that he is King of kings and Lord of lords and that he alone has the right to rule!

Raising the Curtain

The four great powers of the end times are forming before our eyes, and the events of the Campaign of Armageddon seem to loom on the horizon.

Europe is coming together as Daniel and John predicted. Militant Islam is on the rise in the Middle East. The Soviet Union has fallen apart, spawning the birth of six new independent Muslim nations, many of which have nuclear weapons. The world is more at risk of a global holocaust than at any time in history because nuclear weapons are falling into the hands of irrational, fanatical leaders. The fomentation in the Middle East could ignite at any moment into jihad. Moreover, Russia is a wounded, starving bear and is more dangerous than ever before. Vladimir Zhirinovsky is gaining power in Russia, and the entire focus of his political plan is a massive military campaign into the Middle East.

The stage is being set. The events in Ezekiel 38–39 are more imminent than ever before. The consummation of history could begin at any time. All that remains is for the curtain to be raised!

Consider these facts carefully:

1. If the Rapture of the church happened today, the United States could become a second-rate power simply by virtue of the tremendous loss in manpower.
2. The four major powers left in the world would be (1) the newly united Europe, (2) the Muslim world with its oil wealth and the new central Asian allies who have nuclear weapons, (3) Russia, and (4) China and the Far East. These are the four main alignments of nations predicted in the Bible in the last days.
3. As a result of the PLO-Israeli treaty signed on Septem-

ber 13, 1993, and the continued peace negotiations in the Middle East, the covenant with the Antichrist, predicted in Daniel 9:27, seems nearer than ever before.

4. With Israel at peace and living with a false sense of security, the Muslim world will jump at the chance to annihilate Israel and plunder her wealth. Russia is in desperate economic straits, and a leader like Zhirinovsky would jump at the chance to plunder Israel. Gog and his Muslim allies will invade the land of Israel near the middle of the Tribulation period. This invading horde is the rider on the red horse in Revelation 6:3-4 who takes peace from the earth, triggering the Campaign of Armageddon, or World War III, and plunging the world into the great Tribulation.

The raising of the curtain is the Rapture of the church, that great event when our Lord comes to take his bride out of this world before he begins to pour out his wrath on this world (Rev. 3:10). We can see the events of the Tribulation already beginning to line up—the Rapture must be soon!

The questions for all of us to face are: Are we ready? What effect does knowing these truths have on our lives? What's the relationship between Ezekiel and *you?*

THIRTEEN

Ezekiel and You!

THE events in Ezekiel 38–39 will be fulfilled exactly as God has said. The words in these chapters are the very words of God himself. As we have seen the breakup of the Soviet Union and the aftermath of that breakup, I am more convinced than ever before that the events of Ezekiel 38–39 are on the horizon. The stage is being set perfectly for the events we see described in those chapters.

A very important question for every person to consider in light of the information we have received is: What effect does knowing this information have on my relationship with God? Is this simply fascinating, sensational information to tickle our ears and tantalize our minds, or does it have practical value?

Reader Beware!

No one knows how much time they have left on earth, either personally or prophetically. Personally, all of us are painfully aware of our mortality. We have no guarantee we will see tomorrow.

Prophetically, Christ could come at any moment to take his bride, the church, to heaven, and all unbelievers will be left behind to endure the horrors of the coming Tribulation period.

The most important question for every reader to face is whether he or she has a personal relationship with Jesus Christ as Savior. The message of salvation through Jesus Christ is a message that contains both bad news and good news.

The bad news is that the Bible declares that all people, including you and me, are sinful and therefore separated from the Holy God (Isa. 59:2; Rom. 3:23). God is holy and just and cannot just overlook sin. A just payment for the debt must be made.

The Good News, or gospel, is that Jesus Christ has come and satisfied our sin debt. He bore our judgment and paid the price for our sins. He died on the cross for our sins and was raised to life on the third day to show conclusively that the work of salvation had been fully accomplished. Colossians 2:14 says that he "cancelled out the certificate of debt consisting of decrees against us *and* which was hostile to us; and He has taken it out of the way, having nailed it to the cross." 1 Peter 3:18 says, "For Christ also died for sins once for all, *the* just for *the* unjust, in order that He might bring us to God."

The salvation that Christ accomplished for us is available to all through faith in Jesus Christ. Salvation is a free gift that God offers to sinful people who deserve judgment. Won't you receive the gift today? Place your faith and trust in Christ, and in him alone, for your eternal salvation. "Believe in the Lord Jesus, and you shall be saved" (Acts 16:31).

A story is told of a man on Long Island who was able to satisfy a lifelong ambition by purchasing a very fine barometer. When he unpacked the instrument, he was dismayed to find that the needle appeared to be stuck, pointing to the section marked Hurricane. After shaking the barometer vigorously, the man wrote a scorching letter to the store from which he had purchased the instrument and, on his way to his office in New York the next morning, mailed the protest. That evening he returned to Long Island to find not only the barometer missing but his house also. The barometer's needle had been right—there was a hurricane.[91]

The Bible tells us that a hurricane of judgment is coming on our world, and the needle of Bible prophecy today seems to be stuck on the word *hurricane*. Some day soon the Lord will appear to snatch his bride away to heaven, and all unbelievers will be left behind to go through the hurricane of judgment the Bible calls the Tribulation period. Disregard this notice at your own risk.

Believe in the Lord Jesus and flee the wrath to come!

Privilege Brings Responsibility

Those of us who know Christ as our Savior are in a position of great privilege. Do you remember Abraham, the friend of God? Before God destroyed the wicked cities of Sodom and Gomorrah, he came to Abraham and revealed his plan and purpose to his friend. God said, "Shall I hide from Abraham what I am about to do?" (Gen. 18:17). Like Abraham, God has taken us into his confidence and shown us what he will do on this earth in the last days.

What a privilege it is to know the mind of God and to know his prophetic program for the church, Israel, and the nations. However, this privilege brings a heavy responsibility with it. After Daniel received the vision of the ram and the goat in Daniel 8, he was totally devastated: "Then I, Daniel, was exhausted and sick for days. Then I got up again and carried on the king's business; but I was astounded at the vision, and there was none to explain it" (Dan. 8:27). Daniel knew what was coming for his people, and it deeply affected him. There is a heavy price to pay for knowing God's prophetic program for this world. The great privilege of knowing this truth brings an equally great responsibility. Let's look at four of these responsibilities or effects that a proper understanding of prophecy should produce.

Compassion for Sinners

Knowing the truth of Ezekiel 38–39 and the coming Tribulation period should compel every believer to tell lost sinners about Jesus Christ. The thought of people we know and love going through the Tribulation period, not to mention an eternity in hell separated from God, should prompt us to tell them the Good News of the grace of Jesus Christ.

We are reminded in 2 Corinthians 5:20 of our calling during this age: "Therefore, we are ambassadors for Christ, as though God were entreating through us; we beg you on behalf of Christ, be reconciled to God." We are Christ's ambassadors representing him and his interests to a lost and dying world.

Cleansing for Saints

The Word of God is clear that a proper understanding of Bible prophecy should produce a life of holiness. "Beloved, now we are children of God, and it has not appeared as yet what we shall be. We know that, if He should appear, we shall be like Him, because we shall see Him just as He is. And every one who has this hope fixed on Him purifies himself, just as He is pure" (1 John 3:2-3).

Focusing the mind and heart on prophecy, especially Christ's coming, is a fail-safe formula for maintaining personal purity. Note the certainty: "Everyone who has this hope *fixed* on Him purifies himself." Here is a perfect prescription for living a life of holiness: focusing on the coming of Christ. However, his coming must be a reality to us. It is one thing for us to hold right doctrine about Christ's coming. It is another thing for the doctrine to hold us!

In 1988 a man in Oklahoma wrote a book entitled *88 Reasons Why Christ Will Return in 1988*. In the book he alleged that he had conclusive biblical proof that Christ would rapture the church to heaven in early October 1988. The book caused quite a furor in some circles. Of course the Bible declares that date setting concerning the coming of Christ is futile and erroneous (Matt. 24:36; Luke 21:8). However, the book caused many people to reexamine their lives just in case the book was right.

Obviously, the book was totally incorrect, but the point is that, when people began to consider the fact that Christ might return soon, it transforms their lives. The Bible declares that we are to always be looking for Christ's return, not just when some person sets an arbitrary date. "Looking for the blessed hope and the appearing of the glory of our great God and Savior, Christ Jesus" (Titus 2:13).

The practical, cleansing effect of prophecy is also presented in 2 Peter 3:10-14:

> But the day of the Lord will come like a thief, in which the heavens will pass away with a roar and the elements will be destroyed with intense heat, and the earth and its works will be burned up. Since all these things are to be destroyed in this way, what sort of people ought you to be in holy conduct and godliness, looking for and hastening the coming of the day of God, on account of which the heavens will be destroyed by burning, and the elements will melt with intense heat. But according to His promise we are looking for new heavens and a new earth, in which righteousness dwells. Therefore, beloved,

since you look for these things, be diligent to be
found by Him in peace, spotless and blameless.

Now that we know what is coming upon this earth in
the Tribulation period when Gog and his allies invade
Israel, and we see how soon this invasion appears to be,
"what sort of people ought [we] to be in holy conduct
and godliness"?

Comfort for Suffering

Another practical effect of Bible prophecy is that it has a
comforting influence on suffering, sorrowing hearts. In
John 14:1-3 Jesus said, "Let not your heart be troubled;
believe in God, believe also in Me. In My Father's house
are many dwelling places; if it were not so, I would have
told you; for I go to prepare a place for you. And if I go
and prepare a place for you, I will come again, and
receive you to Myself; that where I am, there you may be
also."

The word *troubled* means "to be stirred up, disturbed,
unsettled, or thrown into confusion." There are many
things in our world today to disturb and unsettle us.
Political impotence in our government, crime in the
streets, economic hardship, racial unrest, etc. Added to
these problems are the personal trials and difficulties we
all experience. Trouble is the common denominator of all
mankind. Often these troubles and difficulties of life can
leave us distraught, distracted, and disturbed.

One of the great comforts in times like these is to

remember that our Lord will some day return to take us to be with himself. In John 14:1-3 three points are emphasized—a person, a place, and a promise. The person is of course our Lord, the place is the heavenly city, the New Jerusalem, and the promise is that he will come again to take us to be with him forever.

As we see the events in Ezekiel 38–39 lining up on the horizon, the coming of Christ seems ever so near. Meditating on this truth should give great comfort to us when we are suffering and sorrowing!

Control for Service

The final primary effect that prophecy should have is a controlling influence on serving hearts. In 1 Corinthians 15:58, after presenting the truth of the coming of Christ for his bride, Paul writes, "Therefore, my beloved brethren, be steadfast, immovable, always abounding in the work of the Lord, knowing that your toil is not *in* vain in the Lord."

This verse contains two parts, a negative and a positive. The negative is "be steadfast, immovable." Paul is saying, since you know that Christ will someday come to receive you to himself, let nothing move you, be immobile and motionless. So many today are unstable and unsettled in Christian work. They are constantly vacillating. Knowing about Christ's coming and future events should cure the problem of instability and inconsistency in Christian labor.

The positive is "always abounding in the work of the

Lord." The word *abounding* means "overflowing or over-doing." Another way to translate this is "always giving yourself fully to the work of the Lord." What work has God given you to do? The first two questions Paul asked when he saw the glorified Christ on the road to Damascus were: Who are you, Lord? and What do you want me to do? (Acts 22:8, 10).

Most Christians today have never been past the first question. Most Christians today are spiritually unemployed! We have a spiritual recession in our country to go along with the economic recession.

Martin Luther had two days on his calendar: "today" and "that day." He attempted to live each day in view of "that day," the coming of Christ. This attitude caused him to be a tireless worker for his Lord. Here is a brief summary of three years from his life and his accomplishments: A.D. 1528 (healthy, although one of his daughters died), 190 sermons and lectures, 150 letters, 20 tracts, work on the Old Testament and several trips; 1530 (sick for 10 months), 60 sermons and lectures, 170 letters, 30 tracts, and work on the OT; 1531 (sick for six months, mother died), 180 sermons, lectures, 100 letters, 15 tracts, work on the OT and brief trips.

The principle is clear: Waiters are workers! If the events of Bible prophecy are a reality to us, they will cause us to work faithfully for our Lord. This principle is amplified in 1 Peter 4:7-10: "The end of all things is at hand; therefore, be of sound judgment and sober *spirit* for the purpose of prayer. Above all, keep fervent in your love for one another, because love covers a multitude of sins. Be hospitable to one another without complaint. As each one has received a *special* gift, employ it in serving one another, as good stewards of the manifold grace of God."

May our knowledge of the end times have these effects on us and cause us to heed the words of Jesus: "Be dressed in readiness, and *keep* your lamps alight. And be like men who are waiting for their master when he returns" (Luke 12:35-36). Are you ready?

PROPOSED CHRONOLOGY
OF THE TRIBULATION PERIOD

1. *The Regathering of Israel* (Ezek. 37). It began in 1948, will continue through the first half of the Tribulation period, and will culminate at the second coming of Christ.

2. *The Rapture of the Church* (1 Thess. 4:13-18; Rev. 3:10).

3. *Beginning of the Tribulation*

   A. The Antichrist appears in Europe as an insignificant ruler ("a little horn"). He overthrows three of the kings in the reunited Roman Empire (Dan. 7:8). He is elected to power over the reunited Roman Empire by the leaders of the individual nations (Rev. 17:12-13).

   B. Israel signs a covenant of peace with the Antichrist, the leader of the Western Confederacy (the king of the west) (Dan. 9:27; Rev. 6:2).

   C. The result for Israel is security in the land (Ezek. 38:8, 11, 14).

4. *Middle of the Tribulation*

   A. The king of the south and the king of the north invade Israel (Dan. 11:40; Ezek. 38–39; Rev. 6:3-4).

This is the commencement of the Campaign of Armageddon, or World War III.

B. These two kings under the rule of Gog will be annihilated by God (Ezek. 38–39).

C. The king of the west (the Antichrist) will break his covenant with Israel (Dan. 9:27), enter the Promised Land (Dan 11:40-41), and consolidate his empire by destroying and plundering Egypt, the Sudan, and Libya (Dan. 11:42-43).

D. After his mop-up operation in North Africa, the Antichrist will return to Israel to put down an insurrection there (Dan. 11:44). He will begin his merciless persecution of Israel and will capture and plunder the city of Jerusalem (Dan. 11:45; Zech. 14:1-2; Rev. 11:2). The king of the west will be the political and military ruler of the world (Rev. 13:4).

E. It is at this time that Satan will be cast from heaven (Rev. 12:9-10).

F. The king of the west, or the Antichrist, will set himself up as God, the Abomination of Desolation, in the temple (Dan. 9:27; Matt. 24:15; 2 Thess. 2:4; Rev. 13:5, 15-18). He will rule the world religiously and economically for three and a half years.

G. The Jewish people will flee from the Promised Land amid great persecution (Matt. 24:16-20; Rev. 12:15-17). Unbelieving Israel will be deceived by the false prophet and go into apostasy (Matt. 24:11-12; 2 Thess. 2:11). Believing Israel will proclaim God's message (Matt. 24:14; Rev. 7; 14).

H. Multitudes of Gentiles will be saved and martyred (Rev. 7:9-17).

I. At the middle of the Tribulation, the two witnesses will begin their three-and-a-half-year ministry (Rev. 11:1-14).

J. The seal judgments, numbers two through seven, will all begin just before the middle of the Tribulation, and their effects will carry on through the last half of the Tribulation. All seven of the trumpet judgments will be meted out during the last half of the Tribulation (Rev. 6:3-17; 8:1–9:21; 11:15-19).

5. *The End of the Tribulation*

A. The bowl judgments will be poured out in rapid succession in the final days of the Tribulation (Rev. 16).

B. The great harlot, the city of Rome and the false religious system that prevails there, will be destroyed by the Antichrist (Rev. 17–18).

C. The kings from the east will invade the land of Israel where the Antichrist is headquartered (Rev. 16:12). The armies of the king of the west and the kings from the east will gather at Armageddon to fight one another (Joel 3:9-11; Rev. 16:12-16).

D. The armies gathered to fight will see the sign of the Son of Man in the sky (Matt. 24:30). They will combine their efforts to fight Christ (Ps. 2:2-3; Rev. 19:19).

E. Jesus will return as King of kings and Lord of lords with his army from heaven to slay the gathered armies with the breath of his mouth (Ps. 2:9; Dan. 11:45; Joel 3:12-17; Zech. 14:4; 2 Thess. 2:8; Rev. 19:20-21).

6. *After the Tribulation*

A. The birds are gathered to feed on the carnage at Armageddon (Rev. 19:17-18).

B. Interval period of seventy-five days (Dan. 12:12).

1. Israel regathered (Matt. 24:31).

2. Israel judged (Ezek. 20:30-39; Matt. 24:1-30).

3. Gentiles judged (Matt. 25:31-46).

4. The resurrection of Old Testament and Tribulation believers (Isa. 26:19; Dan. 12:1-3; Rev. 20:4).

7. *The Millennium* (Ezek. 39:21-29; Ezek. 40–48; Rev. 20:1-6).

NOTES

1. Judith Miller, "The Islamic Wave," *New York Times Magazine,* 31 May 1992, 24.
2. Ibid., 23.
3. Ibid., 24.
4. Hal Lindsey and Chuck Missler, *The Magog Factor* (Coeur d'Alene, Idaho, Koinonia House, 1992), 40.
5. Miller, "Islamic Wave," 25.
6. Hal Lindsey, *The Late Great Planet Earth* (Grand Rapids: Zondervan Publishing House, 1970), 63.
7. Louis Bauman, *Russian Events in the Light of Bible Prophecy* (New York: Fleming H. Revell Co., 1942), 23–24.
8. Flavius Josephus, *Antiquities of the Jews,* vol. 1, vi, i.
9. Edwin M. Yamauchi, *Foes from the Northern Frontier* (Grand Rapids: Baker Book House, 1982), 64.
10. Ibid., 101.
11. Ibid., 67.
12. Ibid., 91.
13. Peter T. O'Brien, "Colossians, Philemon," in

Word Biblical Commentary, vol. 44 (Waco: Word, Inc., 1982), 193.

14. Josephus, *Contra Apion,* sec. 38, 2:39.

15. J. F. O. McAllister, "Five New Nations Ask Who Are We?" *Time,* 27 April 1992, 46.

16. Ibid.

17. Ibid.

18. C. I. Scofield, *The Scofield Reference Bible,* 883.

19. C. F. Keil, "Ezekiel, Daniel," in *Commentary On the Old Testament,* trans. James Martin (Grand Rapids: Eerdmans Publishing Company, 1982), 159.

20. Wilhelm Gesenius, *Gesenius' Hebrew & Chaldee Lexicon* (Grand Rapids: Eerdmans Publishing Company, 1949), 752.

21. Donald J. Wiseman, "Rosh," in *The New Bible Dictionary,* 2nd ed. (Wheaton, Ill.: Tyndale House Publishers, 1982), 1040.

22. John Rea, "Rosh," in *The Wycliffe Bible Dictionary* vol. 2 (Chicago: Moody Press, 1975), 1489.

23. T. G. Pinches, "Rosh," in *The International Standard Bible Encyclopedia,* 4 vols. (Grand Rapids: Eerdmans Publishing Company, 1939), 4:2623–2624.

24. G. A. Cooke, *A Critical and Exegetical Commentary on the Book of Ezekiel,* The International Critical Commentary (Edinburgh: T&T Clark, 1936), 408–09.

25. John B. Taylor, *Ezekiel: An Introduction and Com-*

mentary (Downers Grove, Ill.: InterVarsity Press, 1969), 244.

26. Pinches, *Bible Encyclopedia,* 4:2624.

27. George Vernadsky and Michael Karpovich, *A History of Russia,* 3 vols. (New Haven: Yale University Press, 1943), 1:97, 107–108.

28. George Vernadsky, *A History of Russia* (Philadelphia: The Blackiston Company, 1929), 15–16.

29. Bauman, *Russian Events,* 23–24.

30. Rea, *Wycliffe Bible Dictionary,* 2:1489.

31. Jon Ruthven, "Ezekiel's Rosh and Russia: A Connection?" *Bibliotheca Sacra* 25: 332, 1968.

32. Vernadsky and Karpovich, *A History of Russia,* 3:96.

33. Gesenius, *Hebrew & Chaldee,* 862.

34. Ivan Spector, *Russia: A New History* (cited in *Bibliotheca Sacra,* October 1968, 332-333).

35. "The Russia-Iran Connection," *Jerusalem Post,* 21 May 1992, 8.

36. *The Cambridge Ancient History,* 12 vols. (New York: Cambridge University Press), 3:137.

37. T. C. Mitchell, "Meshech," in the *New Bible Dictionary,* 763.

38. Herodotus, *Histories,* 3.94; 7.78.

39. Josephus, *Antiquities,* vol. 1, vi, i.

40. *The Cambridge Ancient History,* 4:195.

41. Francis Brown et al., eds., *The New Brown-Driver-Briggs Hebrew—Lexicon of the Old Testament,* 604.

42. Scofield, *Reference Bible*, 883.

43. *The Cambridge Ancient History*, 3:24.

44. Ibid., 3:55.

45. Brown, *New Hebrew—Lexicon*, 1063.

46. Gesenius, *Hebrew & Chaldee*, 856.

47. *The Cambridge Ancient History*, 4:195; Herodotus, *Histories*, 3.94; 7.78.

48. *The Cambridge Ancient History*, 3:510.

49. Josephus, *Antiquities*, vol. 1, vi, i.

50. *The Cambridge Ancient History*, 3:55.

51. Ibid., vol. 3, map 1.

52. Gesenius, *Hebrew & Chaldee*, 856

53. Brown, *New Hebrew—Lexicon*, 1062.

54. Josephus, *Antiquities*, vol. 1, vi, i.

55. Donald J. Wiseman, "Togarmah," in the *New Bible Dictionary*, 1206.

56. James Wilde, "The Phoenix of Turkish Politics," *Time*, 10 February 1992, 40.

57. Louise Lief, "Fire, Fury and Nationalism," *U.S. News and World Report*, 6 July 1992, 45.

58. "Russia-Iran," *Jerusalem*, 8.

59. Lindsey and Missler, *Magog Factor*, 43.

60. "Russia-Iran," *Jerusalem*, 8.

61. Derek Kidner, *Genesis* (Downers Grove, Ill.: InterVarsity Press, 1967), 107.

62. Pinches, "Cush," in *Bible Encyclopedia*, 2:768.

63. "The Kingdom of Kush," *National Geographic*, November 1990, 98–104.

64. K. A. Kitchen, "Cush," in *The New Bible Diction-*

ary, 256; H. C. Leupold, "Cush," in *The Zondervan Pictorial Dictionary of the Bible* (Grand Rapids: Zondervan Publishing House, 1975), 1:1047.

65. Brown, *New Hebrew—Lexicon,* 468–69.
66. Gesenius, *Hebrew & Chaldee,* 389.
67. John N. Oswalt, *Theological Wordbook of the Old Testament,* ed. R. Laird Harris (Chicago: Moody Press, 1980), 1:435.
68. Miller, "Islamic Wave," 38.
69. Ibid.
70. Ibid., 40.
71. "Color Sudan Islamic Green," *Nation,* 9 July 1990.
72. Michael Georgy, "Christians Face Sudan Crackdown," *Dallas Morning News,* 26 June 1992.
73. Tom Post, "A New Alliance for Terror," *Newsweek,* 24 February 1992, 32.
74. Miller, "Islamic Wave," 40.
75. Gesenius, *Hebrew & Chaldee,* 668.
76. Brown, *New Hebrew—Lexicon,* 806.
77. F. B. Huey, Jr., "Put," in *Zondervan Pictorial,* 4:962.
78. Ibid.
79. Lindsey, *Planet Earth,* 71.
80. Miller, "Islamic Wave."
81. Brown, *New Hebrew—Lexicon,* 1076–77.
82. Gesenius, *Hebrew & Chaldee,* 875.

83. Lehman Strauss, *Daniel* (Neptune, N.J.: Loizeaux Brothers, 1969), 124–25.

84. Thomas S. McCall and Zola Levitt, *The Coming Russian Invasion of Israel,* Updated (Chicago: Moody Press, 1987), 50.

85. H. A. Ironside, *Ezekiel the Prophet* (Neptune, N.J.: Loizeaux Brothers, 1949), 265.

86. A. C. Gaebelein, *The Prophet Ezekiel* (Neptune, N.J.: Loizeaux Brothers, 1918), 252–56.

87. Paul Lee Tan, *Encyclopedia of 7700 Illustrations* (Garland, Texas: Bible Communications, Inc., 1979), 1571.

88. Ibid.

89. David Lawday, "When Allies Leave the Nest," *U.S. News and World Report,* 8 May 1989, 37, 39.

90. Otto Bauernfeind, *Theological Dictionary of the New Testament,* ed. Gerhard Friedrich, trans. Geoffrey W. Bromiley (Grand Rapids: Wm. B. Eerdmans Publishing Company), 6:503.

91. Donald K. Campbell, *Daniel: God's Man in a Secular Society* (Grand Rapids: Discovery House, 1988), 169.